Oh, Baby!

WARNING:

This guide contains differing opinions. Hundreds of heads will not always agree. Advice taken in combination may cause unwanted side effects. Use your head when selecting advice.

Oh, Baby!

Loving (and Surviving!) Your Newborn's First Year

by
Hundreds
of
Happy Parents

Hundreds of Heads Books, LLC

ATLANTA

Cover photograph Michael Blackburn

Cover and book design by Elizabeth Johnsboen

Library of Congress Cataloging-in-Publication Data

Mendelson, Robert A.
   Oh, baby! : loving (and surviving) your newborn's first year / [compiled by Robert A. Mendelson].
       p. cm.
   ISBN-13: 978-1-933512-12-9
   ISBN-10: 1-933512-12-1
   1. Infants. 2. Infants--Care. 3. Parenting. 4. Parent and infant. I. Title.
   HQ774.M458 2007
   649'.122--dc22
                                        2007038769

See page 322 for credits and permissions.

HUNDREDS OF HEADS™ books are available at special discounts when purchased in bulk for premiums or institutional or educational use. Excerpts and custom editions can be created for specific uses. For more information, please email sales@hundredsofheads.com or write to:

HUNDREDS OF HEADS BOOKS, LLC
#230
2221 Peachtree Road, Suite D
Atlanta, Georgia 30309

ISBN-10: 1-933512-12-1
ISBN-13: 978-19335-1212-9

Printed in U.S.A.
10 9 8 7 6 5 4 3 2 1

CONTENTS

INTRODUCTION

Y ou will soon be celebrating three new holidays; Mother's Day, Father's Day and your new baby's birthday. The title of Parent will apply to you. You will be responsible for the well-being of a new member of the family. You are bound to wonder: are we ready? Big decisions and lifestyle changes lie ahead. Your priorities will change.

Unfortunately, babies don't come with an instruction manual. New parents are about to embark on a period of intense OJT (On the Job Training). However, this book will give you an opportunity to learn from hundreds of experienced parents who have been there and done that. Some of their advice will apply to you and your unique situation, and some will not. Consider which suggestions work for you; enjoy reading the others.

All babies are different and *your baby is yours!* You will make the right decisions for your baby and your family. You will receive much advice from many sources. Decide (as a couple) whom to ask for advice: who are the experienced parents you admire? Family members and close friends are often helpful, but you may be treated as if you have no experience (and/or no sense). Learn to graciously ignore unrequested advice without antagonizing the advisor—you might need them to babysit later.

By now your obstetrician has been selected. Now you want to find the pediatrician who will help guide you and your family for the next two decades. Spend time shopping for the best physician. Ask trusted friends and relatives for recommendations. When the same name or pediatric group keeps coming up, make an appointment for a prenatal visit. If possible, both parents should attend, prepared with a long list of questions. Find out all you can about the pediatrician, his/her group, call schedule, practice style, availability in case of emergency, and so forth. Compatibility in this two-decade relationship is most important.

Above all, enjoy this most exciting and challenging time in your life.

—ROBERT A. MENDELSON
M.D., F.A.A.P.

LITTLE HEADS

So you'll know just how expert our parent-respondents really are, we've included their credentials in this book. Look for these icons and numbers:

   👶 = A son   Numeral = age in years except:

   👧 = A daughter   M = Months

   👶-👶 = Twins   W = Weeks

   🤰 = Pregnant

Birth: A Very Special Delivery

Another reason for choosing your pediatrician prior to your due date is that he or she might be needed to help in the unusual event that a pediatrician is needed to help with the baby in the first minutes of life. Most deliveries will go as expected, and your new baby will be placed in your arms with many smiles and congratulations. However, occasionally your obstetrician requests the attendance of a pediatrician at the delivery. This can happen in cases of premature birth (so choose early), multiple births, the need for a cesarean section, or if the obstetrician notices anything that indicates *your baby may be in distress. With modern monitoring technology, fetal distress can be diagnosed early and steps can be taken to minimize risk. Having your pediatrician present to take care of the baby can put your minds at rest. You'll know that everything possible is being done to assure a wonderful outcome.*

ONE OF THE HARDEST PARTS ABOUT HAVING A BABY is actually having the baby. Make sure to scream loudly in jubilation and celebration!

—LOIS
BURIEN, WASHINGTON

MAKE SURE YOU LEAVE EXTRA ROOM for rush hour. There was just nothing more frustrating in the world than being stuck in slow traffic for the birth of our son. Luckily, we still made it to the hospital, but we cut it much closer than we would have liked.

—DEKE
SAN DIEGO, CALIFORNIA
🐵13 🌐10

MY WATER BROKE A MONTH EARLY with our second child. My husband, John, was at the other end of the house in our room. We didn't have anything ready for the hospital. I wandered around the house in a fog putting my bag together, while my husband followed behind me saying, "You don't need that. We have to GO!"

—PAT CURRY
WATKINSVILLE, GEORGIA
🐵17 🐵15

Labor's not as tough as everyone tells you. It was the greatest day of my life.

—M.H.
🌐13M

DELIVERY PLAN

Every well-prepared couple should develop a delivery plan to discuss with their obstetrician during prenatal visits. It is a good idea to prepare this plan during the second trimester (middle three months of the pregnancy) so that changes can be made if appropriate. Here are some decisions that should be made:

1) Who can (and will) be in the labor room with Mom.
2) Type of anesthesia, and use of medications for pain.
3) Location of hospital where baby will be born.
4) Specific preferences of the family and of the parents-to-be.

The obstetrician will discuss the types of deliveries available and what would constitute reasons for a C-section. A meeting of the minds of the doctor and both parents provides peace of mind through this wonderful but sometimes nerve-wracking process.

I HAD PLANNED FROM THE BEGINNING to have a home birth. I was at peace with the idea up until an hour before my daughter was born. At that point I was screaming to be taken to the hospital! But my friend, a midwife, was there, and she reminded me that I wanted a home birth, and to stay true to that. With no regrets, I got what I wanted.

—JEANNE-MARIE CROWE
FAIRFAX, CALIFORNIA
11w

When my wife was in labor with our daughter the doctor said, 'Do you want an epidural?' And I said, 'Yes, I'll take one.'

—EDDIE FINKELSTEIN
CHAPPAQUA, NEW YORK
16 14 9

MY DAUGHTER WAS BORN NINE WEEKS EARLY and I was completely ill-prepared because there were no signs indicating I would have a pre-term baby. In fact, I had ignored the chapters in my baby books that dealt with premature babies. You think it won't happen to you, so you skip those sections. Don't!

—SUZANNE WILLIN
WOODACRE, CALIFORNIA
2

MAKE SURE THAT WHATEVER YOU EAT during labor is yummy (jello, juice, banana) because that's what you're going to taste if you throw up, which I did repeatedly with both kids. Not pretty advice, but I pass it on (unsolicited, of course) to all my pregnant friends.

—D.K.
FOSTER CITY, CALIFORNIA
👩 3 👶 1

. . . .

I think the first time the reality that I was going to be a father hit me was when my wife's water broke. That was when the whole thing sank in.

—TIM
SOUTH PORTLAND, MAINE
👩 7

. . . .

I HAD A SPINAL EPIDURAL and couldn't feel my legs for about twelve hours afterwards. I hated that, so I never did it again. I opted for natural childbirth for the next three.

—LORI T.
CHARLESTON, SOUTH CAROLINA
👶 36 👶 34 👶 31 👶 26

MY WIFE HAD TWO EMERGENCY C-SECTIONS. It was so stressful because I had to choose between following the baby or staying with my wife while they finished the surgery. I chose the baby both times because that's what my wife wanted, but I really wish that we'd had a friend or family member with us to stay with her.

—JERRY B.
NEW YORK, NEW YORK
👶3 👪1

• • • • • • • •

I WAS NERVOUS ABOUT HAVING AN EPIDURAL because people said it slowed labor down, but I really couldn't handle the pain so I did it anyway. The epidural ended up relaxing me so much that it kicked my labor into high gear. I went from four centimeters dilated to ready to push in about an hour.

—MELODY WARNICK
ST. GEORGE, UTAH
👪2

• • • • • • • •

DO NOT LET YOUR BIRTH COACH OUT OF YOUR SIGHT for more than a minute when you're in labor. My husband stepped out to get food and I completely panicked. When he came back, I'd turned into Linda Blair in "The Exorcist."

—DIANA LAWTON
WESTFORD, MASSACHUSETTS
👶2

I always said I didn't care if my baby was a boy or girl, but the second I heard "girl" I was so sure that's what I'd always wanted!

—FRANK
RENO, NEVADA
👪1

GIVING BIRTH AT HOME WAS WONDERFUL. I was able to stay in my own bed and to sleep as much as I wanted after the birth—which was not much, because I kept staring at my new baby in utter astonishment.

—NANCY ENGLISH
PORTLAND, MAINE

. . . .

Drugs are a good thing. When you break your leg, or go to the dentist, they don't say, 'Breathe through the pain.'

—MARET VAN FLEET
ELLICOT CITY, MARYLAND
👶8 👩6

. . . .

I ADVISE ANY MOTHER TO SEND your child to the nursery the first night. The first night she was born, I told the nurses that I was breast-feeding and wanted to have her in the room with me. That was not a very smart decision to make after having a child a couple of hours earlier!

—AMBER WILLIAMSON
COVINGTON, GEORGIA
👩 1

DADS IN THE DELIVERY ROOM: 2B OR NOT 2B

There are pros and cons to having fathers in the delivery room as support and observers of the "blessed event." It is important to discuss this with your OB (your obstetrician) at your first visit to learn her or his opinion. Some OBs aren't comfortable with Dad's presence and strongly discourage (or forbid) his participation, often for medical legal reasons. With that obstetrician, there is no choice. If both parents want Dad in attendance, find an OB who encourages and supports the practice. However, it is a decision to be considered seriously. Some fathers just can't handle observing the process. (As a pediatrician who has attended many deliveries, I have had to resuscitate almost as many fathers as newborns in the delivery room). The dad-to-be or birth coach must be prepared for what he or she is about to see by familiarizing themselves with the stages of birth. They must also be prepared to sit down should lightheadedness or dizziness occur. Fathers who unexpectedly hit the floor can be, and have been, injured.

TIMING IS EVERYTHING

MY WIFE'S CONTRACTIONS BEGAN AROUND MIDNIGHT. At two in the morning we called our midwife for guidance and she told us to wait until the contractions were one to two minutes apart. We timed the contractions with a stopwatch all night, but it wasn't consistent. They would get close together, then spread out again. At eight o'clock we called the doctor's office, and the nurse said the same thing—contractions should be one to two minutes apart. By eleven a.m. my wife had been in labor for nearly 12 hours, so we decided to go to the hospital. I was loading the car when my wife waddled out. She tried to get in the car, and physically could not do it. She realized the baby was coming right then and there. She stood up, lowered her pants, and gave birth to our child in the driveway! One push and he came right out. I ran around the side of the car and the first words my child heard were "Holy shit!" A neighbor called 911, and the paramedics and an ambulance arrived and mother and baby were whisked off to the hospital.

—BRIAN
FT. MYERS, FLORIDA
4 1

MAKE SURE YOUR CAR WORKS! When my wife went into labor, we had a one-hour drive to the hospital. Along the way, I kept noticing my car lights getting dimmer and dimmer until finally, the alternator went out and the car died. At two a.m. I had my pregnant wife in the driver's seat while I pushed our car uphill to the Denny's parking lot so I could call my mom to pick us up. We nearly named our first child Denny because of that experience.

—JOHN COOKE
GREELEY, COLORADO
⊕23 ⚭21

• • • • • • • • •

WE WENT FLYING OVER THE BRIDGE TO PORTLAND with me screaming over every bump. When we got to the hospital the first thing I said was "Oh my God, give me a shot, I can't handle the pain." The doctor examined me and looked at the nurse and said, "Fully!" Meaning fully dilated, move it! I had my daughter an hour later.

—SARAH GOLDBERG
SOUTH PORTLAND, MAINE
⊕16 ⚭8

WE WERE TRAVELING ACROSS COUNTRY from Vermont to California when I went into labor in Utah—two months early. And to make matters worse, we were driving along I-70 where there are signs lining the highway that say "no services," "no rest stops," "no exits." I delivered him at a truck stop along the interstate. Under "place of birth," my son's birth certificate says "Mile Marker 140, I-70E!"

—C.C.
SAN FRANCISCO, CALIFORNIA
1

• • • • • • • • •

I WENT INTO LABOR AROUND 10:00 P.M. The doctor thought I had plenty of time, but I was in serious labor within 15 minutes. We jumped in the car but it was out of gas! We had to stop at a gas station on the way, and I knew the baby was coming right there. We barely made it to the hospital. To this day, I don't know if my doctor made it or if someone else delivered my son!

—NOLA SMITH
TAMPA, FLORIDA
41 35

WHEN I WAS IN LABOR, A NURSE SUGGESTED that doing squats might help me ease the pain during contractions. So when the next one hit, I started doing squats, and counted how many I could do in a contraction—10. The nurse said the contractions would get harder, but not longer. So for the rest of my labor, I knew that when a contraction hit, it would be over in 10 squats. Focusing on counting the squats instead of focusing on the pain helped me get through it. Once I had to be in bed for the delivery, I simply counted my breaths instead. That was the strategy I needed. It eased my labor, and I got through the pain—10 squats at a time!

—ROBYN
BIGLERVILLE, PENNSYLVANIA
1

• • • • • • • •

MY MOTHER WAS A HUGE PAIN IN THE BUTT during labor—constantly asking the nurse what everything was, and she was a nervous wreck, which just made me nervous. Finally, when the time came, I was excited to be able to kick her out of the delivery room!

—ADRIANE
FT. LAUDERDALE, FLORIDA
1

When it comes to childbirth, no matter how much you prepare, you can't know what it will be like until you're in the middle of it. Just be ready for whatever may come.

—JEANNIE
SPONHEIM
LOVELAND,
COLORADO

READY OR NOT!

The day I woke up in labor I was in complete denial about it. Instead of calling my doctor, I decided to go to the movies. My husband kept asking, "Shouldn't you go to the hospital?" But I just waved goodbye and told him I'd call when the time came. Halfway through the movie my contractions got so bad that I left the theater and drove to the doctor's office. I was six centimeters dilated. The doctor told me to call my husband so he could pick me up and drive me to the hospital. I ignored him and instead called my husband and told  him to meet me at the hospital. As I drove myself there, I remember thinking "What a beautiful day." The sky was bright. The sun was sparkling off the snow. I got to the hospital still not thinking that I was really about to give birth. I was prepared to walk the halls and wait for my husband to arrive. But, as soon as the nurse saw me she said "Lie down!" I had my daughter a few minutes later.

—DEB
ORONO, MAINE
18

MY WIFE FOUND THAT IT HELPED HER A LOT if I pushed hard on her hips as she was having the contractions. My arms hurt after a while from all the isometric exercise, but I couldn't very well complain about the pain, now could I!

—FRANK
RENO, NEVADA
1

• • • • • • • • •

Dads, ask the doctor if you can cut the cord when your baby is born. It will make you feel more connected with this tiny new baby.

—M.F.
SAN FRANCISCO, CALIFORNIA
1 M

• • • • • • • • •

CONSIDER GETTING A DOULA to accompany you for the delivery. She is experienced in childbirth, will stick up for your rights as a patient, and can help keep you calm.

—LISA COHEN
BROOKLYN, NEW YORK
7w

A MAN'S PLACE

JUST MAKE SURE YOU'RE THERE. That's the best advice a man can get about surviving the birth of his baby.

—DAVE CASPERSON
WICHITA, KANSAS
👶40 👶37 👶34

• • • • • • • •

YOUR ROLE IN THE DELIVERY ROOM is to get ice chips and rub her back (at least, until the epidural is in). And whatever you do, please don't take anything said by the mother-to-be during labor personally.

—KEITH REGAN
GRAFTON, MASSACHUSETTS
👶5 👶3

• • • • • • • •

DIRECT ALL YOUR ATTENTION TO YOUR WIFE in the delivery room. Breathe deep and look at her reassuringly in the eyes—no matter how much you want to pass out at the sight of all that blood.

—RUSS COX
PORTLAND, MAINE
👶-👶5 👶1

THE BEST THING THAT DADS CAN DO is to just be there, standing, legs slightly bent, ready to run out the door for your wife's every request, as fast as you can. And yes, you must remain in this stance for however long it takes. (I recommend a regimen of squat-thrusts for a few weeks beforehand.) It's almost like the mother-to-be is at a virtual computer, and the dad-to-be is the cursor, and she moves you around the screen. She might click you on the Need A Glass Of Water icon, or the Grab Somebody, I Need Something For The Pain icon.

—DAVID E. LISS
PENNINGTON, NEW JERSEY
🐶4 🐶1

I BROUGHT IN PICTURES OF MY NIECE, who I am completely ga-ga about, to look at while I was in labor. When the pain was at its worst, the pictures really helped me focus, and reminded me that it would all be worth it in the end.

—CeeCee
Reno, Nevada
👶1

* * * * * * * * *

DADS, BE YOUR WIFE'S ADVOCATE IN THE HOSPITAL. Fight for privacy, quiet, whatever she needs, even if it means you have to play the heavy with medical staff and even inquiring relatives.

—Dan Dupont
Arlington, Virginia
👶6 👶3 👶3M

* * * * * * * * *

OUR YOUNGER DAUGHTER WAS BORN PREMATURELY. I left the hospital after 24 hours, but she had to stay for 30 days. It's so horrible to leave the hospital without your baby. Hospital visits were difficult because my older daughter was two at the time, and two-year-olds don't fit in well at the NICU. To make it work, we asked friends and family to come with us to the hospital and sit with our daughter in the waiting room while we visited our baby.

—Kristen
Bethlehem, Pennsylvania
👶3 👶18M

When my doctor asked what kind of childbirth experience I wanted, I told him the same as my mom—they knocked her out and woke her up when it was over.

—Maret Van Fleet
Ellicot City, Maryland
👶8 👶6

HINDSIGHT

We were stationed in Gabon (Africa) when I got pregnant with our first child. We thought about going to Paris (where my husband is from), or the U.S., but I figured women here have babies every day; why should I be any different? So I decided I'd have the baby there. My doctor assured me that they had the necessary equipment should there be any emergency. I had to buy all my own medical supplies—the epidural, saline solution, rubber gloves, etc.

Although our son had a little trouble breathing at first, everything went fine with the birth. But I didn't find out until later, that if there had been a medical emergency, I would have had to fly to France to get to the best facility. It was a frightening realization. I hadn't checked out the clinic enough, and they misrepresented their emergency services. Now I often think of that phrase, "God protects children and fools." I fall into the "fool" category for blissfully, blindly thinking everything should go fine. I would never make a decision like that again.

—A.O.
MARIETTA, GEORGIA
4 2

IN THE HOSPITAL, AFTER HAVING SEVERAL VISITS from family and friends and hospital staff, my husband turned the phone off and set up camp outside of my room. He sat there while I slept for an hour and a half (which seemed like heaven at the time) and would not let anyone in to see me, even the nurses. Needless to say he got away with it for about 90 minutes before they insisted on coming in my room.

—ANGELA STAHL
MILWAUKEE, WISCONSIN
3.5M

. . . .

I decided if I ever have another baby, I will just hire a midwife and have the baby at home. Seems much less theatrical.

—M.F.
CHICAGO, ILLINOIS
1

. . . .

MY HUSBAND HAD THE GALL TO COMPLAIN that he didn't have time to finish the Coke that the nurses had given him in the delivery room because the labor happened so fast.

—GRETCHEN ROBERTS
PALO ALTO, CALIFORNIA
1

WE DIDN'T TURN ON OUR VIDEO CAMERA until after the delivery because I wanted to be a part of the birth, and not a photographer. Instead we got awesome footage of my daughter getting cleaned up, being weighed and measured, and her mother holding her for the first time. They're great shots because my wife was no longer in pain. She was just happy.

> —STEVE MACY
> PARKER, COLORADO
> 2

• • • • • • • • •

OUR DAUGHTER WAS BORN during the 1997 Super Bowl. The home team—the New England Patriots—were in the game so I was less than useful in the delivery room. Doctors came in and out of the room throughout the labor, talking about the game but never saying who was ahead. I would ask, plaintively, from my position in the "cheap seats," who was winning, but no one even acknowledged the question.

> —TIM
> SOUTH PORTLAND, MAINE
> 7

• • • • • • • • •

MY HUSBAND PASSED AROUND CHOCOLATES while I was in labor. The nurses loved him but completely ignored me!

> —LESLIE
> MERRICK, NEW YORK
> 5

For me labor was fantastic. I didn't have to do anything. (I had a surrogate mother.)

—CATHY RAFF
MACCABIM,
ISRAEL
8 5
3

DREAM COME TRUE

When I was pregnant with my fourth, I already had three sons. Whenever we would go anywhere as a family, total strangers would say, "I hope you get a girl this time." I always responded by spouting the usual, "Oh, it doesn't matter to me as long as it's healthy," but I secretly agreed, hoping it would be a girl.

My husband was convinced it would be yet another boy. Whenever I would linger over the pink sleepers and pink dresses and ruffled panties, he would remind me how silly those would look on a boy. As I approached full term, the doctor estimated that the baby could be 10 or 11 pounds—seeming to indicate that it would indeed be a boy.

I was scheduled for a C-section. During the birth I heard the doctor saying, "My gosh, she looks like a three-month-old!" as he lifted our daughter up above the sheet for me and my husband to see. I started crying and said, "I got my little girl!" And Jay held me close and corrected me, "*We* got our little girl."

—ELIZABETH J.
LANSING, MICHIGAN
13 11 8 20M

MY FIRST BABY HAD TO BE SUCTIONED OUT. My second required forceps. The third time around, I was lucky to be paired up with an exceptional nurse, who not only explained every step of the process in great detail, but she told me specifically which muscles to use when I pushed. This made the delivery so much easier and faster. I was like, "Oh, so *that's* how you're supposed to do it!" I can't believe it took me three babies to figure out the correct muscles to use.

> —STEPHANIE ISMERT
> CENTENNIAL, COLORADO
> 👶8 👧6 👶1

· · · · · · · ·

BRING SOMEONE CLOSE TO YOU, other than your husband. At first I felt funny about having another person with me, but I was lying in the hospital bed in agonizing pain, and my husband sat in the chair next to me with his eyes glued to the TV, eating tortilla chips and salsa as if he were at a football party. I knew then I was in big trouble, so my sister-in-law came to the hospital.

> —AUDREY
> LODI, NEW JERSEY
> 👧1

· · · · · · · · ·

HINT TO HUSBANDS WHOSE WIVES ARE IN LABOR: Don't stand around talking to the nurses about sports while your wife has contractions.

> —CATHY K.
> KIRKLAND, WASHINGTON

If you live near a major league ball-park, make sure you have a copy of the home game schedule so you'll know if ball-game traffic will pose a problem or not.

> —LISBETH LEVINE
> CHICAGO,
> ILLINOIS
> 👧6 👶4

WHEN MY WIFE HAD OUR SON, the hospital room and waiting area was filled with my family. It was like a family reunion. Many times the nurses told my family to be quiet: When they wouldn't, they threatened to put them out. That kept them quiet … for a while. During nine hours of labor, my wife couldn't get any rest because my brothers, sisters, nieces, came in one after another to see her. When I went in, she summoned me to come close to her. Then she whispered in my ear and told me to get rid of my family *now* or they would hate her for the rest of their lives. I did what she commanded me to do.

—DEREK WILLIAMS
CHICAGO, ILLINOIS

Have somebody in the delivery room with you, whether it's your mom or your boyfriend or whoever. It helps take the focus off the pain.

—LASHAWNA
GRANADA HILLS, CALIFORNIA

BE CAREFUL IN THE HOSPITAL. They tried to give me the wrong baby—twice! The nurse kept getting confused, and I had to tell her she had the wrong kid. Believe me, though, many times I wish I had kept my mouth shut.

—ADAIR MORELAND
KEARNY, NEW JERSEY

MAKE SURE TO BRING a cute nightgown to the hospital for after the delivery. You get lots of visitors and so many pictures are taken in those first few days, so you'll be glad you did!

—JENNIFER
CINCINNATI, OHIO

Coming Home: The Fourth Trimester

I t's hard to believe that a new mother can be so tired and so excited at the same time. Fatigue is the number one obstacle to enjoying your baby to the maximum. Overtiredness can even manifest itself as what's known as "baby blues," when a new mother feels really sluggish and down. It is so important to get as much rest as possible. If not implemented earlier, this is the time to insist on "visitor control". Ask everyone who wants to visit to please call first to check on the sleep status of baby and parents. It is sometimes necessary to be a little strict with drop-in visitors by saying: "They're asleep right now, and *really need their rest. Why don't you call a little later and come back when they are feeling like company?" This is very difficult, especially for first-time parents, but it is extremely important in the early weeks.*

This is the time when the breast milk supply is being established and it is critical that a nursing mother gets her rest. She should sleep when the baby sleeps, although some babies, bless their hearts, can sleep up to 20 hours each day—although none of my children ever did. Their total activity schedule reads: Sleep, nurse, pee, poop, sleep, nurse, pee, poop … (you get the idea). With a first baby it can take as much as a week or 10 days for the maximum milk supply to be available. If that has gone well, nursing should be a convenient and enjoyable experience for as long as baby and Mom think it is a good idea.

BEFORE HAVING CHILDREN, I HAD NEVER considered myself a maternal person. But then one day you're holding your newborn baby in your arms and it sets in: "Wow, I was made to do this."

> —O.C.
> SAN FRANCISCO, CALIFORNIA
> 5 2

There's nothing more rewarding than a little critter made with half your germs.

—DICKIE
ATLANTA,
GEORGIA
6M

* * * * * * * *

WHEN MY DAUGHTER FIRST CAME HOME from the hospital, it struck me that there were no nurses or doctors to help us care for our baby. At first, this thought instilled panic in me. But then we just did it.

> —SEAN KELLER
> EAST MOLINE, ILLINOIS
> 2

* * * * * * * *

BEFORE I BROUGHT THE BABY HOME, I wish I had known not to take myself too seriously.

> —MARION ROACH
> TROY, NEW YORK

* * * * * * * *

NO ONE GIVES YOU OPERATING instructions on taking this baby home. I spent so much time preparing for the birth, then, all of a sudden they said, "OK, you can take her home." I could've stayed there a month.

> —CYNTHIA
> PORTLAND, MAINE
> 2

MAKE SURE THE CHILD SEAT IS IN THE CAR before the kid is born. My son was a month early and my father-in-law and I had to install the seat in the dark. After we took the baby home, we took the car to the state trooper who inspects baby seats. He just shook his head and said, "You would have been safer just holding him on your lap."

—TOM HARRIS
WAYNESBORO, VIRGINIA
3 1

Mom and Dad should take a break at the same time so that the two of you can spend time together without the baby.

—ANONYMOUS
ALAMEDA, CALIFORNIA
7M

THE NIGHT I BROUGHT MY NEW SON HOME from the hospital my older son said, "We are not as happy as we used to be." When the nurse left, he ran after her crying, "You forgot to take the baby!"

—ANONYMOUS
BALTIMORE, MARYLAND
34 31

WHEN WE BROUGHT OUR SON HOME from the hospital, the most overwhelming thing for us was the sheets and sheets of paper instructing us on how to care for him, feed him, keep him happy and safe. After a couple of months together, we found out that our son teaches us what he needs. When we threw away the pieces of paper and focused on him, it went so much better.

—DAN STUHLFATZ
CONWAY SPRINGS, KANSAS
3

. . . .

ONE BIG THING THAT CHANGES in your life is that you lose spontaneity. But we have wonderful (child-less) friends who come over to our house, to have a great meal and hang out at home. We prefer this to going out because babysitters are $12/hour, so a night out means paying twice—for dinner with your husband and then another $40 to the babysitter.

—MELISSA STEIN
3

. . . .

TAKE CARE OF YOURSELF PHYSICALLY and mentally during this period and don't neglect your needs. Rely on your spouse to do as much as possible. Get on a good health routine as soon as possible. I did, and it worked wonders.

—DAWN RODRIGUEZ
PASSAIC, NEW JERSEY

Take the day off after your child gets his first immunizations.

—JONATHAN AND
JULIANA
ROLLINS
MARIETTA,
GEORGIA
11w

LOVE AT 122ND SIGHT

Do not expect to love your baby wholeheartedly right away. Love at first sight doesn't work with adults, so there's no reason to think it'll work with a newborn. You acquire this blob which doesn't do anything other than cry, eat and poop, and in return you get sleep deprivation, lack of a social life, no sex, and your spouse becoming a whole lot less fun (not that I was a barrel of laughs, either). Honestly, the best part of the day was going to work, where I could look forward to nine to ten hours in a baby-free zone. It probably wasn't until my daughter was four months that I was completely won over by her charm and smile. That's when I really "got into" being a dad.

—MARK KAPLAN
FOSTER CITY, CALIFORNIA
👨3 👶1

I LIKEN THE FIRST THREE MONTHS after childbirth as the "fourth trimester." You get no sleep, you can't predict your schedule, running errands becomes difficult, you can't just pop into the dry cleaners, you have to take the baby everywhere you go. But remember, there is a light at the end of the tunnel.

—T.N.
HUNTINGTON BEACH, CALIFORNIA
👨19M 👶3.5M

SEEK OUT ADVICE FROM PEOPLE YOU RESPECT. In this age of information overload, it's easy to get confused and fearful trying to sort out all the different theories on the right and wrong way to raise children.

—CHERYL PERLITZ
GLENVIEW, ILLINOIS
36 33 31

· · · · · · · ·

Babies are like bowling balls. Unless you're trying, they're a lot harder to break than you think.

—JONATHAN & JULIANA ROLLINS
MARIETTA, GEORGIA
11w

· · · · · · · ·

I HAD MY BABY THE DAY BEFORE MOTHER'S DAY. When I came home from the hospital, there was a card there, in the words of my newborn son. It said things like, thanks for being so healthy and trying so hard while you were pregnant, and thanks for making such good choices for me while I was inside you.

—REINA
HOLLYWOOD, CALIFORNIA
1

Mom is busy taking care of the baby, Dad is busy taking care of Mom.

—D. EVANS
OREGON CITY,
OREGON
8 5

LITTLE HELPERS

INCLUDE OLDER CHILDREN IN THE CARE OF THE BABY. Ask them to help fold clothes. Set an alarm clock and ask them to remind you when it goes off so you know it's time to feed the baby. Compliment them on helping mommy.

—JANET VALLONE
WAYMART, PENNSYLVANIA
34 31 27

· · · · · · · · ·

MY SON WAS FIVE WHEN HIS SISTER WAS BORN. I remember him watching me bathe and dress the baby when I brought her home. He said, "Babies are hard trouble, aren't they?" I got him involved by asking him to be a runner for things I needed. It helped him feel like a big brother.

—ANONYMOUS
RAYMORE, MISSOURI

· · · · · · · · ·

MY DAUGHTER THOUGHT THE BABY WAS HER BABY. He was just a few weeks old when I caught her holding him around the middle, carrying him down the hall. She was way too little to do that—and the baby seemed ill at ease for the rest of the day.

—DOLORES JOHNSON
WICHITA, KANSAS
50 48 45

GIVE THE OLDER SIBLINGS RESPONSIBILITIES with the baby to keep them from getting jealous. My older kids absolutely love helping feed her, hold her, and play with her. Helping their baby sister makes them feel important.

—TABITHA MOTT
CHEYENNE, WYOMING
👩10 👦7 👧5.5M

• • • • • • • • •

I MADE SURE TO CREATE A SENSE of fairness between my children. If I played with my two-year-old, I'd explain, "OK, I've got to take care of the baby now." When I was done with the baby and needed to get back to my older child, I'd tell the baby (in front of my older child, of course), "OK, I've got to take care of your brother now." It created a sense of balance and fairness for my older child.

—KIRSTEN
FORT COLLINS, COLORADO
👦6 👧3

• • • • • • • • •

TIME REALLY IS THE ONLY WAY FOR A CONNECTION to build between a big sibling and a new baby. At first my older son would push the baby away and say, "No." But now, they just love hanging out together and they're inseparable. In the first two years, though, he liked his bunny a lot more.

—ERIC FALKENSTEIN
EDEN PRAIRIE, MINNESOTA
👦5 👦3

FEED THE PARENTS

SEND MEALS TO THE NEW PARENTS' HOME. Mom and Dad won't have time to cook. It's a caring, thoughtful gesture. Parents need that more than they need one more copy of "Goodnight Moon."

—T.P.
LARKSPUR, CALIFORNIA
4

IF ANYONE ASKS WHAT YOU NEED, tell them to bring dinner! New parents have no ability to feed themselves and take care of a newborn. We would have starved to death without the generosity of our friends and family.

—ELIZABETH LEFFERT HEISE
CORAL GABLES, FLORIDA
3M

ONE OF THE BEST GIFTS WE RECEIVED after our first child was born was a gift certificate for a dinner out and a promise of babysitting for the evening.

—KAREN SATHER
DALLAS, TEXAS
7 6

WE WERE TOTALLY OVERWHELMED by having twins. We were first-time parents and we were both learning how to care for two babies and learning how to create a family with twice the need, all in a sleepless stupor. If it were not for our friends, family, church and community who came and quietly fed us, wiped babies' bottoms, and generally looked after the zombie parents, our new little family would not have gotten the wonderful start it did. It didn't take a village; it took a city.

—RUSS COX
PORTLAND, MAINE

Baby care doesn't come naturally for everyone.

—KEVIN SHOLANDER
FORT COLLINS, COLORADO

GIVE ANYONE WHO OFFERS TO HELP specific chores, like put a casserole in your freezer or do a load of wash. It may seem awkward at first, but accepting other people's offers takes the pressure off new parents.

—ANNA LONDON
MELBOURNE, AUSTRALIA

Get a stroller that's practical. Specifically, look for one that isn't too bulky when folded.

—DAVID
SYRACUSE,
NEW YORK

FOR THE FIRST MONTH OR SO I found myself really looking forward to my daughter falling asleep. I would panic when she was awake.

—CYNTHIA
PORTLAND, MAINE
2

• • • • • • • •

MOTHER REALLY DOES KNOW BEST—*your* mother that is! I didn't listen to any of my mother's suggestions for things to buy the baby and she ended up being right. The stroller she bought to keep at her house was nicer, the baby preferred the swing she picked for her house. He even seemed to like the toys she picked more, too. Now I listen when my mom tells me what to buy.

—BRYNN CYNOR
BUFFALO GROVE, ILLINOIS
1

INFANT INFO

During the first few weeks of life, babies can focus on objects eight to twelve inches away. At the end of the first month, most will be able to briefly focus their attention on objects as far away as three feet.

TELL PEOPLE SPECIFICALLY WHAT KIND OF HELP you need. Everyone thought the way to help me was to take the baby. Instead, I would have preferred help with the laundry, cleaning, paying bills, grocery shopping, cooking, grocery shopping again, and countless other tasks.

—SHEENA KROCK
KUNKLETOWN, PENNSYLVANIA
🌐14M

• • • • • • • •

I DROPPED MY BABY THE FIRST DAY she came home! It was a horrible feeling, but she is fine now. Smart, even.

—JENNY B.
NEW YORK, NEW YORK

• • • • • • • •

OUR FIRST SON DID REALLY WELL for a few weeks when we brought his baby brother home from the hospital. Then, all of a sudden, he decided that he wanted to wear diapers, too, even though he'd been potty trained for months. He also wanted to go back to a bottle, just like the baby. I worried when it persisted, but the doctor said to let him wear diapers again (I drew the line at a bottle). He said, "His friends are eventually going to notice he's wearing diapers. They'll make fun of him and it'll stop." That's exactly what happened.

—ANONYMOUS
GAMBRILLS, MARYLAND
🌐38 🌐36 🌐30

SLINGS ARE THE GREATEST INVENTION for the crucial "fourth trimester." I wore my daughter six to eight hours a day. Whenever my daughter would cry, I'd stick her in the sling and walk around. She'd usually go to sleep.

—BRITT STROMBERG
CAMANO ISLAND, WASHINGTON
11M

WE SHOULD HAVE REALIZED THAT the personality differences between our parents/in-laws and us would not disappear with the bliss of cuddling cute little babies. On the contrary, the differences became heightened in the face of total sleep deprivation and crying, colic-stricken babies, and this created stress on top of stress. When the grandparents are only visiting to hold and feed one of the babies during daytime hours, this really does little to help the parents. The grandparents, of twin grandbabies especially, should be prepared to help with the cooking, cleaning, and even nighttime duty if their visit is meant to be any relief to the parents.

—A.A.
CONNECTICUT
3

BUY A SLING! Women have been carrying babies across their chests for centuries.

—DENISE
JASPER, INDIANA
9 6 1

EVERYONE'S A CRITIC

IF SOMEONE GIVES YOU UNSOLICITED ADVICE, ignore them.

—ANONYMOUS
NEW YORK, NEW YORK
9M

• • • • • • • •

LITTLE OLD LADIES ALWAYS THOUGHT MY SON LOOKED COLD
no matter how bundled up he was. I just smiled patiently. I
figure one day I'll be the little old lady dispensing advice
just for an excuse to come fuss over a baby!

—DAWN
COLUMBUS, OHIO
7 4M

• • • • • • • •

UNSOLICITED COMMENTS ABOUT YOUR BABY can seem
presumptuous, but sometimes a stranger can notice
things that you might not. One time a woman on the bus
told me that my son was very observant,
saying, "That kid's taking in everything." She noticed what a genius my
son was before I did!

—JOAN
NEW YORK, NEW YORK
32

BABY'S BEST FRIEND

ALWAYS SUPERVISE PETS WITH A BABY. Even the most trusted pet can accidentally harm a child. We put a screen door on the bedroom which allowed us to hear our daughter if she cried, and let fresh air circulate, while not letting our cat have access to the baby's room.

—ERIN BROWN CONROY
SCHOOLCRAFT, MICHIGAN

WHEN MY DAUGHTER WAS BORN, we rubbed a blanket all over her and took it home for the dog to smell and play with. That way, when she came home, our dog wasn't sniffing her and going crazy with a new person in our home.

—CHRISTINE GALLAGHER
NARBERTH, PENNSYLVANIA
4M

WHEN THE BABY CAME HOME, our cat started having real territorial problems and started spraying in every room. He sprayed all over the baby's toys! We tried a number of things to help him, including hiring a cat "therapist" who advised giving him antidepressants. We ended up giving our cat away.

—A.C.
SOUTH PORTLAND, MAINE
5

I WAS ALWAYS TOLD TO SMEAR PEANUT BUTTER on a new baby's toes and let the dog lick it off. (Not too much peanut butter, mind you, or the dog might forget there are toes under there!) I passed this advice on to my sons when they had kids of their own, and they said it worked like a charm.

—VERA PETTY
BEAUMONT, TEXAS

. . . .

I'D HEARD THAT CATS SOMETIMES LEAP into a baby's crib and hurt the baby, so we kept a careful eye on our two cats. In turn they kept an eye on the baby. We have pictures of each cat sitting on the windowsill studying the baby as if they were keeping watch over him. I actually think Ficha and Fuzzy took the baby in stride better than we did.

—LINDA ANDREWS REEVES
SAN ANTONIO, TEXAS
10 5

. . . .

A DOG TRAINER ONCE TOLD US THAT THE FIRST YEAR, you protect the baby from the dog. But once your child starts to walk, you need to protect the dog from the baby.

—SUE RODMAN
ATLANTA, GEORGIA
6 4

OUR CAT WAS A KITTEN WHEN OUR BABY WAS BORN so really they grew up together. That's the best way to avoid jealousy on the kid's or pet's part!

—BEV PORTER
COLORADO SPRINGS, COLORADO
14 🐾11

• • • • • • • • •

WITH OUR FIRST SON, OUR DOG ACTUALLY SAT in the corner for about two weeks, pouting. We made sure to pet her and play with her while holding our son, so she knew that he wasn't taking all her attention away, and we tried to keep her on her usual schedule so she wouldn't think we forgot her. Gradually the dog came around and now they are the best of friends.

—MICHELLE M.
OOSTBURG, WISCONSIN
😊2 😊2M

• • • • • • • • •

WHEN MY BABY WAS BORN, I wrapped him in a blanket, then gave the blanket to my husband to take home for the dogs to sniff. The dogs slept with the blanket until I came home from the hospital. This way, my dog recognized the baby's scent when we came home.

—ANONYMOUS
STOWE, VERMONT
😊 2

MAKE YOUR CHILD AN ACTIVE PART of your lifestyle. You might not realize that they actually like going to the bank or the grocery store with you. Take the baby with you because not only will it make your life easier, you'll get in some serious bonding time.

—TESS DIXON
CORALVILLE, IOWA
👧4 👶17M

• • • • • • • •

THE FIRST TIME I GAVE MY DAUGHTER A BATH, I almost drowned her. She was in her little baby tub, and I was so exhausted that I must have relaxed my elbow, and my baby's face went under the water. Thank goodness, my husband noticed, yelled, and I pulled our baby's head out of the water. She did some sputtering, but she was just fine.

—ROSANNA
NEW YORK, NEW YORK
👧 👶

• • • • • • • •

MY MOTHER WAS A GODSEND in helping me get sleep because she stays up late and gets up early. If I was tired or awakened early and felt too sleepy to handle the baby, my mother would already be up and waiting when I took the baby to her.

—MONICA AND TODD DENNIS
BRIDGEPORT, CONNECTICUT
👶4 👧6M

Don't let your compulsion to do everything perfectly turn you into someone who tries to do it all alone. I wish I could have found, and accepted, more help.

—NANCY ENGLISH
PORTLAND, MAINE

SINCE HAVING A BABY, starting a conversation between me and my husband is difficult because we're either too busy or too tired. I miss having conversations with my husband so now we're making an effort to talk while the baby sleeps.

—CAMILLE FREDRICKSON
BRUSSELS, BELGIUM
4.5M

DON'T BOTHER WITH FANCY BATHTUBS for your newborn. Babies are so tiny, all they need is a little plastic tub or the sink itself. I recommend always having your baby sit on a washcloth to help prevent slipping. Babies are very, very slippery!

—JENNY W.
NEW YORK, NEW YORK
4

BEFORE MY FIRST CHILD WAS BORN, I was working full-time. I thought I'd keep working and get my master's degree, too, with the baby just "fitting in." After the baby was born, everything changed. I hadn't counted on falling in love with this little person and wanting to spend all my time with the baby!

—ANDREA LARSON
FORT COLLINS, COLORADO
12 9

DOUBLE YOUR FUN

TWINS SHARE A SPECIAL BOND. Let them sleep in the same crib. Even as newborns our twins needed to be together. If we laid them down on opposite ends of the crib they'd end up with their feet touching each other. If they didn't feel each other they'd start crying.

—PAM BOEA
SYRACUSE, NEW YORK
🧒19 👶17 👶-🧒15 🧒12

• • • • • • • • •

HAVING TWINS WAS A LOT EASIER than having one child. Twins amuse each other from a very young age. With a single child, you spend a lot more time trying to keep them happy.

—KELLY DIXON
KIRKLAND, WASHINGTON
🧒23 👶-👶16

• • • • • • • • •

THE BEST ADVICE WE GOT from other parents of twins was to be ruthless about keeping them on the same schedule. When one would wake up to eat, we'd always wake the other and feed him, too. Otherwise we would never get a break from the feeding, rocking and changing schedule.

—HILLARY
MADEIRA, OHIO
👶 8 👶-👶 3 🧒 11

MOTHERHOOD CHANGED ME FOR THE BETTER

I GREW UP WHEN I HAD A BABY. I used to be "wild," but as a mother I felt I needed to be a responsible adult. Sometimes I miss the old times, but as long as my children are small I feel that I need to be available and fully functioning at all times.

—HEIDE A.W. KAMINSKI
TECUMSEH, MICHIGAN
18 15 6

HAVING A BABY MADE ME MUCH MORE conservative in my actions. I took fewer personal risks. I became more interested in politics and society, as I wanted to have a good society for her to live in. I became more involved with my extended family. I thought more about the choices I made to set a good example for her. I also worried a lot more.

—CLAIRE YURDIN
SEATTLE, WASHINGTON
26

EVERYTHING I DO NOW IS FOR MY CHILD, where before it was mostly for myself. I wouldn't have it any other way.

—P.J.
HAVRE DE GRACE, MARYLAND
2

THE OTHER NIGHT, OUR FRIENDS WERE HEADING into the
city for an art opening, and there I was, waving
goodbye—barefoot, in my sundress, one
boob out, and a child hanging on me!
I'm in a very different place now than I
was before.

> —M. DeJong
> FAIRFAX, CALIFORNIA
> 5w

I WAS 22 WHEN MY FIRST DAUGHTER WAS BORN, and a
softness developed in me. I became softer and I treated
people better. You just see things differently when you
have a child. A lot of women say that they don't want to
have kids and they're not ready for children. I always tell
them that will change when they are pregnant. When
you get pregnant, you might be scared, but you're
already in love.

> —LILLIE MARIE CUTTER
> STONE MOUNTAIN, GEORGIA
> 22 24 37

MY GOALS CHANGED WHEN I had kids because I wanted
the best for my kids. My goal became to get a job and
work hard to support them.

> —LUNCINO TONIQUE RIVERA
> JONESBORO, GEORGIA
> 7 6 1

I WAS A NOTORIOUS PROCRASTINATOR. No more. Now, if I have four hours to work, that's it. It's got to get done then. I've also learned to accept things as "good enough." Very hard, since I was a perfectionist.

—BRITT STROMBERG
CAMANO ISLAND, WASHINGTON
11M

- - - - - - - -

SHARING WORK WAS DIVIDE-AND-CONQUER with a baby in the house. She cooks. He cleans. She does laundry. He does dishes. He does it his way. She does it hers. No questions, as long as it gets done. In our house Dad does baths. Dad reads. Dad puts the kids to bed. This is "daddy time." Mom feeds at night and Dad does the rest (dressing, bathing, diapers, singing, etc.).

—JUDITH WONG
MILWAUKEE, WISCONSIN
5 2 4M

- - - - - - - -

FOR YOUR BABY'S SAKE, SLOW DOWN for at least the first six months. With our first child, I had the attitude that nothing in my life needed to change—we could still do all the things we did before. And we did. But it wasn't so good for the baby. By the second child, I learned to slow down and adjust to the baby's schedule. You just have to accept that this is a phase and remember that it won't last forever.

—LISA
WINDSOR, COLORADO
16 13

One of the everyday benefits of having a baby is you meet lots of new parents. It is a whole new world.

—SKYE FERRANTE
NEW YORK,
NEW YORK

BABIES ARE NOT SWEATY AND STINKY like adults. Mostly, you just need to wash off anything they've spit up before it turns sour. A sponge bath for the first few weeks is sufficient. Too much bathing is not good for their skin.

—MARTY
CHICAGO, ILLINOIS
17 15

- - - - - - - -

I know a lot of people may say this, but I mean it: There's really no way I could have made it through those early days without my husband!

—HILLARY
MADEIRA, OHIO
1 3 8 11

- - - - - - - -

THE BABY SLING REALLY HELPED OUR SON SLEEP, which let us get a lot more done. At first I didn't want to wear one because they either looked too hippie or too girlie. But I've learned that if it works, you wear it. If it's pink, you wear it. It'll have throw-up on it sooner or later anyway.

—GUY ADAMSON
CONNECTICUT
14M

DRESS FOR SUCCESS

I HAVE A GRIEVANCE ABOUT THE SNAPS. When you are so sleep-deprived and your baby is kicking and screaming, it is the hardest thing in the world to get those snaps inside the leg to line up properly! They should be color coded, to help ensure proper matching and reduce frustration.

—K.H.
FAIRFAX, CALIFORNIA
5.5M

• • • • • • • • •

I'M WONDERING IF IT'S POSSIBLE FOR BABY CLOTHING designers to make it more difficult to dress and undress a baby. Buttons? Are you kidding? On a squirmy baby? And 57 snaps for one pair of bottoms? Or how about the full-body suit? Whose bright idea was that for poopy baby? It's like a practical joke. As I struggled with my babies' clothing while they cried and tried to wriggle free, I kept thinking a TV host would pop out and yell, "Gotcha! We were secretly videotaping you to see just how ridiculous you'd look trying to fasten 27 hook-buttons, a line of Velcro and all those snaps." Unfortunately, that never happened.

—JWAIII
ATLANTA, GEORGIA
5 2

MAKE SURE TO DRESS YOUR BABY in dorky little clothes with silly bunny ears and tails and that sort of thing. It's the only time in your life you'll have such complete control over what they wear, and it's funny! We took pictures and now that they're teens, it's great to break out the photos and embarrass them.

—JILL H.
NEW YORK, NEW YORK
14   12

• • • • • • • •

ALL BABY CLOTHES ARE PRETTY darn cute if you ask me, but the first time I saw my infant son in a teeny-tiny Ohio State football jersey, I nearly melted!

—CHRIS ANDRUSS
CINCINNATI, OHIO
5   7   1

PLACE YOUR BABY TO NAP IN A BABY SWING when you need to take a shower (within your eyesight, of course). Both baby and parent will feel rested and better.

—C. KARP
IRVINE, CALIFORNIA
👶 4

> *I did not take enough time off when I left the hospital. I needed more time to bond and rest before working again.*
>
> —DAWN RODRIGUEZ
> PASSAIC, NEW JERSEY

• • • • • • • •

YOU SEE YOURSELVES AS "PARTNERS" before the kids come, but afterwards we became one mom and one dad with distinct roles.

—DEANA KRAUSE
CHICAGO, ILLINOIS
👶 11 👶 9

• • • • • • • •

"SHOPPING" MEANS BUYING THE SAME dress in four different colors before your little one cries, wets herself, gets tired or—by age one—tries to climb out of the stroller.

—CASSANDRA FOX
FAIRFAX STATION, VIRGINIA
👶 18 👶 15

• • • • • • • •

DON'T BE CONCERNED about your house looking perfect. Your baby doesn't care how your house looks.

—NORA HAMMOND
LOUISVILLE, KENTUCKY
👶 39 👶 35

MY LIFE DEFINITELY CHANGED when I had my first son. I had to wake up in the middle of the night. I also had to get a job to support him. Surprisingly, I didn't mind waking up in the middle of the night; I was so excited that I was his mother that it didn't really bother me.

—AUDRIANNA JOHNSON
CONYERS, GEORGIA
1   2

The sweetest moment was when I brought my baby home and finally got the chance to be alone with her. My husband was at work, his family had left, my family had left, and it was just the two of us.

—AMY GILLIAM
MILFORD, OHIO
1

ACCEPT ALL THE ASSISTANCE YOU CAN GET. As long as you show appreciation, the grandparents don't mind helping.

—SUETTA GRIFFITH
FISHERSVILLE, VIRGINIA
33   31

NECESSARY OBJECTS

DON'T BUY CUTE COVERS FOR THE CHANGING PADS. It's so much easier when you can just wipe down the pad itself, which has a plastic exterior.

—TONY T.
SAN FRANCISCO, CALIFORNIA
6M

· · · · · · · · ·

I WOULD ADVISE PARENTS TO NOT WASTE MONEY on things like bassinettes and fancy crib bumpers when they won't get used for long, if at all. Our son insists on sleeping with us for at least half the night, and he always has, so we could have saved ourselves $300 and purchased a used crib instead of a fancy new one.

—DEANN ROSSETTI
MAPLE VALLEY, WASHINGTON
4

· · · · · · · · ·

THE ONE THING YOU ALWAYS NEED to have with you is a plastic bag. In fact, you should have a stash of them in the stroller, car, and your bag. You never know when you'll need to bag up a dirty diaper, smelly bib, or half-eaten banana. They're especially useful when you're on a plane and your seat is covered in garbage.

—LORI B.
CHARLESTON, SOUTH CAROLINA
19 16 13 3

YOU SHOULD DEFINITELY BUY A SWING-O-MATIC, because when the baby is crying and nothing makes the baby happy, the Swing-O-Matic will. It is kind of depressing because the baby likes the Swing-O-Matic better than you! But you'll get over that.

—BILL W.
SEATTLE, WASHINGTON
🐣26 🐣23

. . . .

BUY TWO COVERS FOR YOUR CHANGING PAD. This way you can have one in the wash and use the other.

—CAROL GILMORE
EASTON, PENNSYLVANIA
🐣6

. . . .

EVERY MOTHER NEEDS TO HAVE A BABY SWING. We call it the Neglect-O-Matic.

—SHARON LONDON
SAN FRANCISCO, CALIFORNIA
😊42 🐣40

. . . .

MY FAVORITE PIECE OF BABY EQUIPMENT is cloth diapers, not for diapering the baby but for bleach-able cleaning up of unspeakable baby messes.

—MELODY PHILLIPS
SARATOGA SPRINGS, NEW YORK
😊17 🐣16

THE TOUGHEST TRANSITION, after I had my first child, was being responsible for somebody else and giving up what I wanted to do to take care of my child.

—SHAWNA N. RUSSELL
SACRAMENTO, CALIFORNIA
3 4 10

* * * * * * * *

I HAD MY DAUGHTER WHEN I was a medical resident so I was still doing night calls and had to be in the hospital for 36 hours on certain days. The hardest thing was feeling that I had to be an adequate mother and physician. I've said many times that I had a nervous breakdown that year. I also had to find a child care provider for her—someone that would watch her the way I would. I felt if I could make it through that year I could survive anything.

—DEBORAH W. YOUNG
LITHONIA, GEORGIA
22 25

* * * * * * * *

SOON AFTER I CAME HOME FROM THE HOSPITAL, I got in my car and started driving to the grocery store. I suddenly remembered that I had a baby and she was asleep by herself inside the house! I immediately turned the car home and ran inside to check on her. She was safe, but I was a wreck. I sat down on my bed and started crying.

—ANONYMOUS
NEW YORK, NEW YORK
4

Being a stay-at-home mom was the biggest change for me after I had my daughter; I've been working since I was 14.

*–NIEEMA TURIYA PEYREFITTE
HAWTHORNE, CALIFORNIA
1*

MUST-HAVES

- **A CAR SEAT:** Use it every time the baby travels in an automobile, including the trip home from the hospital. The car seat must be approved for your infant/child and placed in the middle of the back seat facing backward until the baby weighs 20 pounds.

- **AN ACCURATE THERMOMETER (AND THE KNOWLEDGE TO USE IT):** There are many kinds of temperature measuring devices. In the first year, the rectal thermometer is the most accurate. After six months, the ear thermometer may be used.

- **ACETAMINOPHEN DROPS TO TREAT PAIN OR FEVER:** The best-known brand is Tylenol®. Ibuprofen (Motrin/Advil) is also effective, but should be used only as a backup because it can upset the stomach.

- **HAND SANITIZER:** but soap and water will do.

- **A FEW COTTON,** washable outfits with diaper access (and a good supply of diapers).

- **CHILD-PROOF ENVIRONMENT** for the baby's safety

- **SMOKE-FREE ENVIRONMENT:** If parents smoke, they should quit. If they can't quit, smoke only outside—never smoke in an enclosed place where the baby may be, including in the car.

OH, HOW I LOVED THAT SLING! I'd tuck my son in there and we'd walk all over, trying not to chuckle at all the other moms maneuvering bulky strollers through tiny store aisles.

—STEPHANIE WOLFE
GROTON, CONNECTICUT
23M

Don't despair when you realize that not every moment is filled with joy. In those moments, know that it's true what other moms say: It really does get easier and better.

—ELIZABETH
GAINESVILLE, FLORIDA
1

THE BIGGEST CHANGE WHEN I had my daughter was not having time to do the things that I normally did. Your social life changes immediately when you have a child; you have to learn how to make time for yourself.

—LINDA VANESSA HILL
ATLANTA, GEORGIA
24   21

BREAST IS BEST!

A few important decisions should be made by the parents-to-be during the last few months of pregnancy. One is whether to feed your baby breast milk or formula. Pediatricians (including the American Academy of Pediatrics) recommend breast-feeding exclusively for the first six months of life and then the gradual introduction of solid foods. While this is ideal, modifications may be made depending on your family situation. Breast-feeding for any length of time is better than none. Breast-feeding and slow and late introduction of solid foods is especially important in families with a history of allergies. Discuss the subject with your pediatrician. You may be referred to a lactation specialist or a breast-feeding support group. They can be especially helpful to the "rookie" family. Everyone has an opinion about breast-feeding, and if nursing is possible, it is in the best interest of the baby. Having said that, a baby is able to grow and thrive without being breast-fed or on a combination of breast milk and formula. Sometimes a woman is unable to breast-feed; this does not make you a bad mother. Consider your options and make the best choice for your baby and your family.

WHAT YOU DON'T NEED FOR A NEWBORN

It is not necessary to have a lot of equipment at home at the beginning. Aside from a place to sleep (which could be a bassinet, small crib, or Moses basket, for example); a washable, soft pad on which to change diapers; and a comfortable place to bathe, babies don't really need much. Full-size cribs, bouncy chairs, swings, and so forth, can all be obtained later when the baby is developmentally ready. And many of these items can be found as hand-me-downs.

I WAS ALONE WATCHING MY SON when a friend called and invited me to his house. Without even thinking, I said that I would be there in fifteen minutes. I put on some shorts, grabbed my wallet and keys, and was out the door. As I drove down the street I suddenly realized that I had a baby. I raced back home, called my friend, and cancelled. I was just so used to my life being a certain way. It took several weeks for me to realize that I was really a father with responsibilities to someone else other than myself.

—RICK
HOUSTON, TEXAS
1

THE HARDEST PART FOR ME was not just the lack of sleep, but the lack of consecutive hours of sleep. Everybody told me that I wasn't going to get much sleep in the beginning, which was fine and I was prepared for it. But not getting more than two hours at a time was really hard! I remember how excited I was the first time I got four hours in a row after my daughter was born—I felt like a new person!

—JENNIFER SHINN
MARIEMONT, OHIO
1

. . . .

THE TOUGHEST THING ABOUT THE FIRST THREE MONTHS is the lack of sleep, but there are definitely ways to help deal with it. We were really lucky because both my parents and my husband's came over and helped us out in the beginning. If you can get help during the day, it'll really help you deal better with the nights.

—JENNIFER
CINCINNATI, OHIO
1 2

. . . .

MY DAUGHTER HAD COLIC FOR WEEKS. Our pediatrician had only one therapeutic suggestion to make: alcohol and plenty of it, for the parents.

—RALEIGH MAYER
NEW YORK CITY, NEW YORK
10

Start really early with the sling; it takes a lot of work to get your baby used to it.

*–J.V.
LOS ANGELES,
CALIFORNIA
1*

BARE BABY ESSENTIALS

There are the obvious necessities: diapers, formula, crib, etc. And then there are all the froufrou items found in the infants department. What newborn really needs a portable diaper-changing table? Won't there always be a place to change the baby? Do I really have to have a diaper stacker? These are the types of questions you'll want to ask yourself while shopping around.

New moms quickly learn that some of their first-trimester purchases, like wiper-warming machines and cereal caddies, will only be used once or twice, if ever. That's why it's important to try to limit your purchases to the basics. Clutter is one thing every new mother can live without!

The following is a list of essentials:

- Bottles, nipples, and a bottle brush (if not breast-feeding)
- Diapers (newborn size, but don't buy too many packs—babies grow fast!)
- Diaper bag
- Wipes (you can never buy too many of these)
- A good supply of at least eight light blankets and a couple of baby quilts
- Pacifiers and more pacifiers

- Baby lotion and baby soap
- Hooded towels
- Tiny nail clippers
- Cornstarch-based baby powder
- Baby bathtub (though the kitchen sink works just fine)
- Spare crib sheets
- Seasonally appropriate clothing (buy larger sizes than the tags say—a three-month-old baby will probably not wear size 0-3 months)
- Infant carrier/car seat
- Baby swing (this is a lifesaver and the best invention of man ... or, probably, woman!)
- And finally, expensive bubble bath (for you! You will deserve it.)

—JOANNA YOUNG
OKLAHOMA CITY, OKLAHOMA
15 10 6 12

DURING MY BABY'S FIRST THREE MONTHS I started going back to school and my husband went back to Iraq. So I was by myself, and I was breast-feeding. During those months I was not getting enough sleep, my breasts were engorged, and I was missing my baby. I had to deal with the fact that I was not going to get the sleep that I needed and I was going to be a single parent until my husband returned. That was very tough.

—AMBER WILLIAMSON
COVINGTON, GEORGIA
1

Babies are wiggly little things and need neck and head support all the time, so don't under-estimate that!

*—JENNY B.
NEW YORK,
NEW YORK*

THE HARDEST PART OF THE FIRST THREE MONTHS was trying to figure out which cry meant what. It takes some time, but if you listen closely, you can hear when the baby wants different things, like food, sleep or a cuddle. Then you can give them just what they need.

—MANDY PARROT
LOVELAND, OHIO
5 - 1

MAKE SURE YOU HAVE A HELPER AROUND, whether it's a friend, nanny, mother-in-law or a doula—anyone who will offer you unconditional support and will not criticize your choices or methods.

—D. EVANS
OREGON CITY, OREGON
8 5

THE SLEEP LOSS IS DEFINITELY the hardest part of the first three months. I know everybody advises this, and almost as many people laugh at it, but I really did sleep when the baby slept, and it helped a lot during those long nights when no one was sleeping.

—SHELLY
CINCINNATI, OHIO

Parenting certainly expanded me. It questioned me. It challenged me. It's a new kind of love.

—MARION ROACH
TROY, NEW YORK

THE TOUGHEST THING ABOUT THE FIRST THREE MONTHS was nursing. At night, my baby wants to nurse constantly: she wasn't hungry but it made her comfortable. I had one of those bouncy exercise balls: one night, I sat on it while holding my daughter and started bouncing. She fell asleep right away and I was able to put her in her crib and get some sleep myself.

—LILY
DIX HILLS, NEW YORK

THE HARDEST PART OF THAT FIRST THREE MONTHS was adjusting to the isolation of not being at work and around lots of other people. So I started to work a bit from home, and I sought out other people in a similar situation, so I had a new network of people around me.

—VANESSA
LIBERTY TOWNSHIP, OHIO

TOOLS OF THE TRADE

THE WORST PIECE OF EQUIPMENT I tried was the Maya wrap. I hated it! It was really difficult to wear properly and my daughter didn't like being in it. I spent hours trying to make it comfortable. I even went online to get advice from other mothers, but I could never get it right.

—DANIELLE
ORANGE, CALIFORNIA
👧 1

• • • • • • • •

I BOUGHT A WRAP, but I had a really hard time figuring out how to position my daughter in it. It was always too loose or too tight and she would always fall to one side and make me think she was going to fall out.

—MARLA
BURBANK, CALIFORNIA
👧 1 👧 3

• • • • • • • •

THE PORTABLE PLAYPEN is one the piece of equipment that gives my husband the most trouble. He has a very short temper with plastic, so whenever we need to take it somewhere, I put it together and he carries it.

—MARY WALSH
CINCINNATI, OHIO
👶 1 👶 4 👶 6 👧 7

MY STROLLER WAS A HUGE DISASTER. I couldn't figure out
how to work it, so I threw it on the ground in a fit of
rage; little plastic pieces of stroller went flying. For a new
mom, there is enough to figure out—the equipment
should be easy.

> —ANONYMOUS
> NEW YORK, NEW YORK
> 🧑4

• • • • • • • •

WE BOUGHT WAY TOO MUCH STUFF. One day I realized we
had seven strollers! I thought we needed the jogging
stroller, the regular everyday stroller, the umbrella stroller
for quick trips to the store, and so on. But we really didn't.

> —VANESSA
> LIBERTY TOWNSHIP, OHIO
> 🧑1 🌐3

• • • • • • • •

I BOUGHT HUNDREDS OF CLOTHES and before my daughter could fit half of what we bought, she grew out of
them. There were still tags on the clothes, and the store
allowed me to bring the clothes back and exhange them
for bigger sizes. Next time, I won't buy so much.

> —SHERITA TOLEDO
> CHICAGO, ILLINOIS
> 🧑1

WHEN MY WIFE AND I PREPARED for our baby's first bath, it took both of us to do it—one to hold the camera and the instruction book, and the other to actually bathe the baby.

—KEVIN SHOLANDER
FORT COLLINS, COLORADO
🐾 12 👶 10

• • • • • • • •

DON'T HIRE A BABY NURSE—it will just undermine your confidence as a new mom.

—ELIZABETH LEFFERT HEISE
CORAL GABLES, FLORIDA
🐾 3M

Topsy Turvy: Feeding & Cleaning

The first months at home are a learning experience for the baby and the new parents. A good way to think about it is that the baby is "not quite done" and major maturation of the senses occurs rapidly during this time. Your baby's vision, hearing, and responsiveness improve in amazing leaps and bounds. Rapid growth accompanies all of these changes; your baby (and you) will be very different after the "fourth trimester." This is a time of settling in for both of you. You will become more comfortable with each other. Activities of daily living such as bathing, diaper changing, feeding, etc. will all be *much smoother, easier, and part of a routine that you and your baby will love. During this time of getting used to each other, make sure your baby spends a great deal of one-on-one time with each parent as well as "family" time with both parents. Mom and Dad also need some one-on-one time with each other to communicate the joys (and not so joyful things) about parenthood. It's very important not to lose touch with your spouse during this period of adjustment.*

WHEN NURSING YOUR BABY, no matter where you are or what you're doing, try to look right into those precious eyes and savor the moment. That bond is something which will last forever.

—BRIGITTE THOMPSON
🐵10 🐵6 🐵2

• • • • • • • •

EXPECTANT PARENTS SHOULD READ up on nursing, and maybe even keep the number of the local La Leche League handy. I really studied up on the whole pregnancy and childbirth thing but for some reason I thought nursing

would be a no-brainer. Wrong! My first son had problems feeding. As an exhausted first-time mom it was especially hard to deal with.

—VICKY MLYNIEC
LOS GATOS, CALIFORNIA
🐵19 🐵15

• • • • • • • •

I PRACTICED BREASTFEEDING AT HOME with some really good friends over before I tried nursing in public. I figured if I accidentally flashed them or just got flustered, we could all laugh about it.

—DENISE
BOSTON, MASSACHUSETTS
🐵4 🐵1

Breastfeeding is unlike any other bond—so much stems from the emotion alone.

—DENISE
JASPER,
INDIANA
🐵9 🐵6
🐵1

I BREASTFED FOR THE FIRST YEAR AND LOVED IT. It allowed me to develop a relationship with my baby that wouldn't have been achieved with formula or pumping. It also gave her the necessary nutrients and antibodies she needed that only I could give.

—E. HIRSH
WEST PALM BEACH, FLORIDA
7

• • • • • • • •

Use formula to supplement breastfeeding. It gives you a break.

—JESSICA VAUGHAN
RANDOLPH, VERMONT
10 8 6 4

• • • • • • • •

I RECOMMEND BREASTFEEDING FOR THE FIRST YEAR. Why? I lost my pregnancy weight faster. I don't get my period while I'm breastfeeding. My son rarely gets sick because it's boosted his immune system. It's free. It's always available when my baby is hungry. My baby never smelled like formula. And breast milk is what human babies are meant to eat!

—MICHELLE BELT
EDGEWATER, MARYLAND
4 3M

IN THE BEGINNING, BREASTFEEDING HURTS. It hurts, it hurts. Your nipples are sore, crusty, bloody, and for the first few weeks they feel like they are going to fall off. Even though the books say the baby has to be sucking the right way and latch on and all that crap, it doesn't matter. Your breasts have never had the likes of a baby's suck on it, no matter what strange boyfriends you may have had in the past. If you really want to breastfeed, grin and bear it and it will get better. It's all worth it in the end.

—ANONYMOUS
SINGER ISLAND, FLORIDA
1

. . . .

THE FIRST COUPLE OF WEEKS OF BREASTFEEDING really hurt. I mean really. So make a pact to stick it out for three weeks to a month. Then, if you still hate it, you can always switch to bottles. But most likely, you'll have gotten past the bad period and will start to appreciate how convenient it is, and what a great chance it is to comfort, feed, and bond at the same time.

—K.T.
BURLINGTON, VERMONT
5 4 1

. . . .

YOU DON'T HAVE TO BREASTFEED if you don't want to. Your child will survive, and you will, too.

—L.S.
SHARON, MASSACHUSETTS
5 4

> *Make sure you have a good pump— don't be stingy!—so that you're not always bound to the baby.*
>
> *—ANONYMOUS*
> *AUSTIN, TEXAS*
> *6*

STRONG WORDS

DO YOUR RESEARCH ON THE BENEFITS OF BREASTFEEDING.
Everyone talks about it being a "choice," but if you
spend a moment comparing formula to breast milk, there
is no contest. To give a child formula is almost criminal
considering it contains so many harmful preservatives, is
so difficult for a tiny baby to digest, and
does not build your child's immune system.

—ELIZABETH LEFFERT HEISE
CORAL GABLES, FLORIDA
3M

DON'T BE AFRAID TO ADMIT THAT YOU DON'T WANT to
have a child attached to your breast 24/7. If it were as natural as everybody tells you it is, why are there "lactation
consultants" to teach him/her how to "latch on?" If it were
natural, he/she would come out knowing how to nurse.

—ANONYMOUS
BROOKLYN, NEW YORK
2

THERE IS NOTHING WRONG WITH FORMULA. You will not
be a bad mom if you give your baby formula. If you're
happy, your baby will be happy.

—ANONYMOUS
STOWE, VERMONT
2

I WAS AGAINST BREASTFEEDING. I thought it was so gross to have another human being latched on all the time. Then I became pregnant and all of a sudden I was all about breastfeeding. I became a huge advocate for it and encouraged all my family and friends to breastfeed. I have no idea what changed my mind . . . maybe the hormones!

—LESLIE BUNDY
WAUKESHA, WISCONSIN
👶1

• • • • • • • •

I HAD TROUBLE NURSING MY NEWBORN because I was not producing enough milk. I remember calling a lactation consultant and was told to keep trying, drink lots of water, eat well, and get plenty of rest (yeah, right). By the time my son went for his one-month visit, he was on the lowest end of the scale for weight gain. I tried the same routine for a few more weeks. My son was miserable at every nursing. I was a mess. We would both cry through it. I finally decided to put him on formula. What a world of difference! He was gaining weight well and we were both happy at feedings. It was like I had a whole new baby!

—SHEENA KROCK
KUNKLETOWN, PENNSYLVANIA
👶14M

People become much more tolerant of nursing in public once they hear the baby screaming for a few minutes.

—RACHEL RINO
CHAPEL HILL,
NORTH
CAROLINA

FROM THE SIDELINES

SMART HUSBANDS SHOULD URGE THEIR WIVES to continue nursing for as long as possible, because as long as they're nursing they're the only ones who can deal with nighttime feedings. As far as I'm concerned, kids can continue to nurse until they're 18 years old.

—JOEL ROSENFELD
NEW YORK, NEW YORK
☺-👶17 👶15

• • • • • • • •

IF THE WIFE'S IN CHARGE OF INPUT, the husband's in charge of output!

—JUDY CONNERS
WICHITA, KANSAS
👶40 👶37 👶34

• • • • • • • •

I'M AGAINST NURSING. I think it's important to share all those fun and not-so-fun responsibilities. I liked getting up in the middle of the night, changing diapers, watching them sleep, babysitting and caring for them. I would've been disappointed not to have had those opportunities.

—KEN BLAISE
DIABLO, CALIFORNIA
👶26

MY WIFE BREASTFED, would not pump, and did not want to feed the baby formula. I felt helpless at times, and I was concerned the baby didn't know who I was. Then I realized that I was there to read, go on walks, play, and make faces. Now, at a year old, our daughter still fusses almost every time my wife changes or feeds her. With me, everything is a game to her—she is good as gold and laughs when I take care of her.

—MARC A. CLAYBON
GOLDEN, COLORADO
15M

IF YOU INTEND TO BREASTFEED, line up a lactation consultant before you give birth—get tips beforehand and attend a breastfeeding support group. I assumed it would all "come naturally," but it's not easy. I was up 24 hours a day with sore everything until I found a lactation consultant who saved my little family!

—ELIZABETH LEFFERT HEISE
CORAL GABLES, FLORIDA
3M

• • • • • • • •

Breastfeeding is very hard at first, but it's wonderful in the long run. Pregnant women should be told about the health benefits of breastfeeding—for baby and for mother.

—MARRIT INGMAN
AUSTIN, TEXAS
2

• • • • • • • •

FORMULA ISN'T POISON, despite what some women say. I fed my son my breast milk for almost six months, but then switched to formula. My son is now a perfectly healthy, happy and smart four-year-old. He is perfect—tall for his age, lean and lanky, smart and healthy.

—DEANN ROSSETTI
MAPLE VALLEY, WASHINGTON
4

BOTTLED MILK CAN BE SERVED at room temperature—it doesn't need to be heated on the stove or in the microwave. Each night, we'd put three batches of formula on a tray, along with three bottles already filled with liners and water. When our daughter woke up, we dumped one batch of formula into the bottle, shook it up, and were ready to go. It saved all that time of going downstairs and heating up the bottle, so all of us could go back to sleep that much sooner.

—GAIL MANGINELLI
SCOTTSDALE, ARIZONA

• • • • • • • •

I CALLED A LACTACTON CONSULTANT FOR ADVICE when I was fretting about how to breastfeed my triplets. She said to take out a calendar, call everyone you know and get people to come over and help you every day because you can't do it by yourself. I had women coming over from my church that I had never met! It was the best advice anyone could have given me because for the first three months I was feeding babies every 30 minutes, 24/7.

—CHRISTIE PATRICK
ATLANTA, GEORGIA
👶-👶-👶 8M

• • • • • • • • •

I CAN DISTILL MOTHERHOOD DOWN TO ONE LINE: When in doubt, nurse; if that doesn't work, give Tylenol (once the doctor says it's OK, of course).

—RACHEL RUVO
CHAPEL HILL, NORTH CAROLINA

Breast pumps don't work! I tried both battery-powered and manual pumps. I sprayed milk all over the room!

—M.S.
TORONTO,
CANADA
👧 11 👧 9
👦 7

WAYS TO WEAN

WEAN YOUR CHILDREN EARLY. It's much harder the longer you wait. My daughter is two and a half and I have been unable to stop nursing, even though I want to. I thought, in the very beginning, she and I would know together when it was time to stop. Now I want my body back; I'm physically ready but she's not emotionally ready.

—CYNTHIA
PORTLAND, MAINE
2

• • • • • • • •

I TIMED MY BREASTFEEDING TO STOP when I went back to work. I have a job that means I am in a lot of meetings so I can't always get away to pump. I made sure I started weaning before I went back to work, not after.

—JULIE KIND
ARLINGTON, VIRGINIA
6M

• • • • • • • •

WHEN YOU'RE WEANING A BABY FROM NURSING, it's the night feedings that are hardest to stop.

—K.B.
SAN FRANCISCO, CALIFORNIA
6 3 3M

I BREASTFED, BUT I DID NOT HAVE ENOUGH MILK to feed
her completely, so I combined breastfeeding and bottle-
feeding, which worked well for us. She weaned herself
from the breast and then continued with the bottle alone.

—CLAIRE YURDIN
SEATTLE, WASHINGTON
26

• • • • • • • •

STOP NURSING WHEN THE CHILD IS READY. With my first, I
totally believed the doctor and went cold turkey at 12
months. It broke my heart and, in retrospect, he wasn't
fully ready. With my second I nursed for 18 months and
when I weaned him he was ready.

—THERESA
WICHITA, KANSAS
7 5

BREAST-FEEDING WAS THE HARDEST PART of my baby's first year. I wish doctors and writers would be honest about the intense pain that many women experience, and offer real advice without making women feel abnormal.

—ANONYMOUS
LOS ANGELES, CALIFORNIA
🙂 3

• • • • • • • • •

THIS IS THE BEST ADVICE I GOT ABOUT FEEDING twins: First, if you are breastfeeding, assign one breast to each child and always stick with that.

Second, when one wakes up, always wake the other up and feed them at the same time. This helps to get them on a schedule.

Third, when they are on solid food, just use one spoon for the both of them. One bite for this one, then one bite for that one.

—CELINE SWANSON
KIRKLAND, WASHINGTON
🙂 10 🙂-😊 6

INFANT INFO

Studies show that breastfed babies are less likely to be under- or overweight and are less susceptible to disease than formula-fed babies.

IF YOU'RE NOT ONE OF THOSE WOMEN who feels comfortable whipping out their boobs in public, do what I did: Have a "breastfeeding cape" made. It's a big piece of fabric with a hole cut out for your head, and a few buttons in the front. I could slip it over my head and nurse comfortably and discreetly in public, and still peek in to see how the baby was doing.

—ANONYMOUS
CHARLESTON, SOUTH CAROLINA
5

MY SON WAS COLICKY AND REALLY GASSY. As he was nursing, he would suck and then cry. My friend thought he might be congested, so we put some saline drops in his nose and he cleared right up. He was able to nurse after that.

—MELANIE WILLIAMS
ATLANTA, GEORGIA
4

NO MATTER WHAT SOMEONE—and that someone will likely be your mother-in-law—says, don't ever stick your finger in a baby's diaper to see if it's dirty. I tried it and got a nasty surprise. It's far better to take the time to unsnap all the snaps on their outfit.

—RUSSELL LISSAU
ARLINGTON HEIGHTS, ILLINOIS
2

You hear that breast milk doesn't stain—it does.

—MARYBETH
SAN FRANCISCO,
CALIFORNIA
4

THAT FIRST BATH

Giving your baby that first bath at home can be a joyful experience for the bather and the bathee. It can also be frightening if you haven't done it before. If this is the case, ask an experienced parent, grandparent, or friend to help you. The goal is simple: get the baby clean in water of the appropriate temperature while constantly supporting the head. The water should be body temperature. (You can use a thermometer, but dropping a few drops of water on the inner surface of your forearm works just as well. The water should feel neither hot nor cold—that means it's body temperature.) Use any mild soap, a soft washcloth, and lots of loving and cooing. For the hair (if there is any), soap or a baby shampoo can be used and rinsed out quickly. Try to avoid getting any soap into the baby's eyes. Wash the face gently with the soft cloth and work your way down the rest of the body. The genitalia is a little tricky (girls' are trickier than boys') but don't try to remove all the whitish, gooey secretion. This secretion is a natural protection for the baby girl's vagina and labia. Washing it too briskly can also be uncomfortable. Try to finish the bath in as a short time as possible so the water won't cool too much. Wrap the baby in a soft towel, find a comfortable chair, and enjoy each other for some time. See, you are now an accomplished baby bather!

MY HUSBAND AND I HAVE A GAME. The last person to put
a finger to his or her nose has to change the diaper.
We've found our hand-nose coordination has really sharp-
ened the last few years.

—ALEXIS KLEINHANS

• • • • • • • • •

*Changing a diaper isn't brain surgery.
Men have a tendency to make things
harder than they really are. Just lay the
baby down, untape the diaper and wipe
them clean. Put a new one on, and voila!
You're done!*

—STEVEN GREEN
LOS ANGELES, CALIFORNIA
35 30 29 25 17

• • • • • • • • •

NURSING IS THE GREATEST SURVIVAL TOOL to parenting and
the best thing you can do for your baby. I loved the sensu-
ality and closeness of it and the ability to comfort my child.

—JENNIFER TAYLOR ATANDA
ALEXANDRIA, VIRGINIA
2

KEEP SPARE DIAPERS IN A FEW PLACES, not just your diaper bag. Diapers are small, so I just put one in my regular purse, one in the glove compartment, one in my husband's computer bag for work, one in the stroller pocket. These emergency stashes have come in handy a couple times.

—CHRISTINE B.
NEW YORK, NEW YORK
👶4M

THERE ARE SOME DISPOSABLE DIAPERS, like Tushies, that aren't made with all those artificial chemicals and plastic by-products against the baby's skin. I think it has cut down on rashes. It just seems more natural and better for her than the other ones.

—CARL M.
MINNEAPOLIS, MINNESOTA
👶1

Get a hair dryer. If you use a hair dryer after you change a diaper and wipe the baby down, there is no diaper rash.

—WILLEM KNIBBE
ALAMEDA,
CALIFORNIA
👶7M

TRY USING CLOTH DIAPERS DURING THE DAY, and disposables at night. Cloth diapers are better for the environment, and they are no more expensive or difficult than disposables. They are better for the baby, too, because he or she will only have cotton against their skin and not that plasticy, chemically stuff. Plus a cloth diaper service will deliver clean diapers and pick up the dirties.

—SAM
SANTA MONICA, CALIFORNIA
👶13 👶1

FOR BOYS, REMEMBER TO ALWAYS, I mean *always*, have a diaper cloth, burp rag, towel, or clothes from the hamper in your hand during the diaper change. I got sprayed a few times before I learned that lesson.

—C.H.
LOS ANGELES, CALIFORNIA
6 4 1

I can't imagine how older generations made it without disposable diapers. I know they're bad for the environment, but they save oodles of time and make this job much more bearable.

—DAVE BAUDER
CROTON-ON-HUDSON, NEW YORK
5 3

BUY THE RIGHT DIAPER BAG. It's worth the money, considering you're going to be carrying it for a year or two. And some of them look so great that you can use them as carry-ons later.

—DAWN
COLUMBUS, OHIO
7 4M

YOUR FIRST DIAPER

CHANGING YOUR FIRST DIRTY DIAPER can easily become one of those sweaty, tension-filled, bomb-defusing situations in which you're yelling for your spouse to help but he can't hear because the baby's wailing at the top of its lungs and your hands are shaking and there's runny yellow poop all over the half-unsnapped onesie, and the baby's face is turning purple and you don't know yet that that's what babies look like when they poop.

Just keep this in mind: Nothing is as frightening as that initial poopy diaper and in no time at all you become so unfazed by this, and a whole lot more.

—KRISTEN RAMSEY
LOS ANGELES, CALIFORNIA
🐶 3

• • • • • • • • •

MY NEWBORN DAUGHTER'S NURSE WARNED ME that it might take her a while to start going to the bathroom. Two days later…well, it was like Niagara Falls! I guess things had really backed up! My biggest mistake is that I had put her in cloth diapers. I should've made sure she was sealed up really good, like with disposables AND plastic pants.

—RACHEL WALASKAY
SEDALIA, COLORADO
🐶 11 🐶 8

AFTER GIVING BIRTH TO MY SON, my friend was with me at the hospital, and she helped me change his diaper for the first time. As soon as he had his diaper off he started to pee. I was so surprised that I picked him up carried him around the room, asking my friend, "What do I do?!" Needless to say I made a big mess. That's when the nurse walked in and said, "Ladies, when you're changing his diaper, have a clean diaper ready to cover his penis."

> —SARAH GOLDBERG
> SOUTH PORTLAND, MAINE
> 🌐16 👣8

• • • • • • • •

GIRLS HAVE LOTS OF NOOKS AND CRANNIES; they're like an English muffin. There's a zillion folds in there. With boys, when the air hits them, they pee. So, as soon you open the diaper, you drop a tissue on him and cover it up.

> —EDDIE FINKELSTEIN
> CHAPPAQUA, NEW YORK
> 👣16 🌐14 👣9

• • • • • • • •

COMPLAIN ALL YOU WANT about having to change diapers, but I am grateful to be a mom after the invention of disposable diapers. My own mother had to use safety pins on cloth diapers that she had to launder herself. Now *that's* something to complain about.

> —MISSY
> DETROIT, MICHIGAN
> 🌐14 🌐12 👣9

> *Poop. Get used to it. It becomes part of your life, and conversation about it lasts a lot longer than you want.*
>
> —ALEXIS KLEINHANS

RATHER THAN CARRYING DIAPER changing supplies around the house, create diaper "stations." I put a basket with two or three diapers, wipes, and ointment in every room of my house. Literally every room—the dining room, living room, master bedroom. This way, I didn't have to lug things around, and changing diapers didn't become an interruption.

—JEANNIE SPONHEIM
LOVELAND, COLORADO

* * * * * * * *

FOR HYPER CHILDREN, take the following steps while changing diapers:
1. Have all your supplies ready.
2. Before the diaper is off, have a big wad of wipes at hand.
3. Give the baby a favorite toy to hold on to (this will keep her attention for about five seconds).

—JULIE BAJUSZ
SAN ANTONIO, TEXAS
7 5

* * * * * * * *

CLOTH DIAPERS SEEM LIKE A GREAT IDEA because they are wonderful for the environment. The problem is, you have to buy the wraps which are very expensive. Plus, washing them, even if you use a diaper service, is very time consuming.

—ISABELLA BAUHAUS
SANTA CRUZ, CALIFORNIA
18M

I nursed my daughter for two and a half months. Nursing can help you lose weight, and it is the best milk for your baby.

—TANYA ROCHELLE
SHERMAN OAKS,
CALIFORNIA
1

DIAPER GENIES ARE GREAT BUT THE REFILLS are expensive.
Buy a separate trash can and cheap liners (from
Costco) for those pee-pee diapers and throw the
liners out every other day. Use the diaper genie
for the stinky poo-poo diapers.

> —ANONYMOUS
> AUSTIN, TEXAS
> 21M

*Always keep a change of clothes for
yourself and baby, especially during the
baby's first year when messes (and
leaks!) are more likely to occur.*

> —J.L.
> MIAMI, FLORIDA
> 6

IF YOU HAVE DOGS, MAKE SURE YOU CLOSE the door to
the baby's room when you leave the house. Dogs like to
eat dirty diapers.

> —JWAIII
> ATLANTA, GEORGIA
> 5 2

BE PREPARED

Murphy's Law: The worst diaper emergencies occur when you are least prepared to deal with them. If you think you can slip in a five-minute trip to the store without the diaper bag, or go anywhere and forget the diaper bag, that's when disaster will surely strike.

Create an emergency kit for the car (extra diapers, lots of wipes, a blanket that you don't mind getting dirty and lots of extra plastic bags for disposal). Remember, you can never have enough diapers. If you think you'll need three, take five.

—KEITH REGAN
GRAFTON, MASSACHUSETTS
5 3

IF YOU SHOW EXTREME ENTHUSIASM for changing a diaper, your baby will appreciate it and you'll have fun, too. I made up a song to sing to my daughter whenever it was my turn to change her diaper. When my daughter was older and more alert, she'd start singing the song with me. It made diaper changing so much more efficient, because she was distracted by the song (and my singing). When my son was born, we sang the song to him. "The Poopy Diaper Song," as it became known, is now a part of family lore.

—JWAIII
ATLANTA, GEORGIA
5 2

OH, BOY!

IF YOU HAVE BOYS, CHANGE THE DIAPER FAST. And never lay a baby on an expensive Persian rug in your husband's boss's home.

> —LISA ARMONY
> SHERMAN OAKS, CALIFORNIA
> 5 2

IF IT'S A BOY, USE TWO DIAPERS. Use one to cover up his business, because he is going to pee again, just as soon as you pull that wet diaper off and the cold air hits him. It's like that old camp trick where you put someone's hand in water while they are sleeping.

> —CLIFF JOHNSON
> WICHITA, KANSAS
> 50 48 45

THIS IS KIND OF GROSS, but you should really avoid talking when you change a baby boy's diaper. They squirt and when that little hose goes off, you want to make sure you have your mouth closed. It only happened to me once, but it was horrible.

> —ANGIE GUILLEN
> LYTLE, TEXAS
> 23M

PLAY GAMES AND ENTERTAIN YOUR BABY while changing her diaper. If that doesn't work, prepare to gut it out. I sang songs. I played "This little piggy . . ." I made kissing noises. I would go through different body parts, and end by tickling her—anything to make the experience more fun.

—L.O.
SYRACUSE, NEW YORK
3 1

USE THE FORCE

Gentlemen, heed my advice: Be the Diaper Jedi. To begin, master the dual leg lift—with one hand, grasp both ankles in a single clutch. Fold the front of the diaper back over the poop to create an absorbent but temporary workspace under the baby's dirty, wiggly butt. Wipe the area clean, leaving nothing behind. If your station is properly set up, a tube of rash cream is on hand, ready to go. With practice, you'll flip the cap and squeeze a dab on your finger with the flair of lighting a Zippo. All the while you are singing out loud, distracting the kid. A new song every time. File away the favorites for "code red" situations when your newborn turns into a kicking, screaming brat. May the force be with you.

—A.L.
SAN FRANCISCO, CALIFORNIA
13M

USE A HAIR DRYER AT THE CHANGING TABLE. Not only does it provide heat and air to keep baby dry and warm (if you let them air dry you run the risk of a fountain!) but the "white noise" of a hair dryer on "low" also soothes them. As soon as our son would start to fuss, the hair dryer went on and he was instantly calmed and comforted.

—PAM IVALDI
DUBLIN, CALIFORNIA
4M

Some days, you just have to hold your breath.

—CAROLE
NEW YORK, NEW YORK
2

I REMEMBER OUR FIRST BIG POOP EXPLOSION. I was running late, and as soon as I put my son in the car seat, boom! Poop everywhere. It was all over him and all over his seat. I started crying, and then he started crying. I took him out of the car seat, changed him and cancelled my appointment. There is only so much a mom can handle.

—ANONYMOUS
PHOENIX, ARIZONA
1 4

Babies have perfect skin naturally and smell delicious— well, once the crap is cleaned off of them.

—SAM
SANTA MONICA, CALIFORNIA
13 1

MY NEPHEW'S DIRTY DIAPERS WERE THE MOST powerfully overwhelming, repugnant things I have ever encountered. One night while babysitting, I was changing him in the bathroom, and had him in the tub for thorough cleaning. I had the bathroom window open so I could breathe a little, and suddenly my husband came running in the room, took the dirty diaper and sailed it out the window. He said, "I'm sorry, honey, I just couldn't have that thing in the house one more second." So I had to go find it and put it in an outside trashcan.

—KATHY PENTON
SAVANNAH, GEORGIA
23

YOU DON'T HAVE TO CHANGE THE BABY'S DIAPER if s/he is not wet. Diapers are highly absorbent, and a little liquid is not going to mandate a full changing.

—MELISSA STEIN
3

INFANT INFO

It takes approximately 500 years for a disposable diaper to break down in a landfill.

WE WERE ON A ROAD TRIP and we stopped to change my son. I handed my husband a bag with a dirty diaper and asked him to throw it away; he threw it in the trunk instead. A few days later my car started to smell but I couldn't figure out where it was coming from. I brought my car to the detail shop to hopefully resolve the problem smell. When I picked up the car, someone from the shop told me that they found a bag of dirty diapers in the trunk under some bags.

—ANONYMOUS
VAN NUYS, CALIFORNIA
2

. . . .

DON'T WAIT WHEN IT COMES to getting your baby used to water. Pour small amounts of water over your baby's head from their very first bath. That way he or she will grow up to like water, swimming, and bath time!

—AMY
CINCINNATI, OHIO
3 1

. . . .

STRUGGLING WITH BREAST-FEEDING? Try not to make it a big deal if it's not working out. Say to yourself, "Today is a good day, even if tomorrow won't be," or, "Maybe today we can just feed on this side and not on the other."

—REBECCA
DENVER, COLORADO
1

Learn how to diaper a baby the "normal" way and also in a face-down position. When they start crawling around, this skill comes in handy.

—C.H.
LOS ANGELES,
CALIFORNIA
6 4
1

ESCAPE ARTIST

Anyone who's had a baby knows that keeping a diaper on your little bundle of joy can be tough. Once they learn how to take off those Velcro straps, it's clear sailing from then on. You've tried everything, and the little one is still streaking through the house multiple times a day.

There is a way to solve this problem. Take a trip out to your local hardware store and pick up a roll of the best $2 solution to diaper escaping you can buy: Duct tape! Here's what you do (after you finish laughing at this). Take a piece of regular duct tape and rip it in half lengthwise, so it's thinner than it was. Then, wrap the duct tape around the front of the diaper, covering both of the Velcro tabs. Make sure the piece is long enough to reach all the way around to the back of the diaper. If you do this in the opposite way, your little escape artist will figure out how to take the tape off. If the ends are around the back, they won't have enough dexterity and strength at that angle to get them off.

—Dan Pasquale
Modesto, California
😊3 🐣5 🐣2

EVERYONE SEEMS TO MAKE breast-feeding out to be this beautiful, earthy, natural thing that is nothing but bliss. It is all of those things, of course, but it also hurts—a lot! Even if you're doing it right! I was surprised that no one prepared me for that.

—MANDY HUECKER
MAINEVILLE, OHIO
😊4 👶2

• • • • • • • •

INVEST IN AN ELECTRIC BREAST PUMP. I was able to get out every now and then, since the baby could be bottle-fed with the same nutrients I provided, and being cooped up all day long can drive one crazy, and it allowed other people in the baby's life to experience the joy of feeding an infant .

—LEA ACHIVIDA
SAN DIEGO, CALIFORNIA
👶7

• • • • • • • •

GET THAT BABY ON A SCHEDULE as soon as you can. I had my daughter on a feeding schedule at six weeks and it made life so much easier. I always knew she would eat at 2:00, 5:00, 8:00 and 11:00, so I could plan the other things I needed to do around it. Plus, if you can get them on a feeding schedule, a sleeping schedule falls in line with it.

—WENDY
LOVELAND, OHIO
😊7 😊5 😊1

I figure that if I'm near a baby and holding a diaper bag that I automatically look cool because people love to see an involved father.

—BRETT
COLUMBUS, OHIO
😊7 👶4M

ALL SYSTEMS ARE "GO"

You will be amazed at how frequently your baby pees and (later) poops. Some babies pee and poop after every feeding! If so, it certainly means your baby is getting enough to eat. You can expect at least 4-5 pees every day and 1-3 poops every day. After the first few weeks, a breast-fed baby may poop much less frequently (even as little as once a week). If nursing is still going well and there are lots of wet diapers, it means that almost all of the mother's milk is being used for nutrition and growth and there is little waste (another advantage of breast-feeding). Don't worry; after solids are introduced, there will be plenty of poops!

Obviously, new parents will have to get comfortable with changing wet and dirty diapers. Again, if you feel you could use some help, call on experienced parents you trust for advice and instruction. It is your choice whether you use disposable or cloth diapers. (Hint: A month or so of pre-paid diaper service is a wonderful gift for new parents.)

ONE TIME I WAS OUT WITH MY SON and he pooped all over himself. I had no idea what to do until I saw a garden hose outside someone's house. I turned it on and put my son's bottom under the hose and cleaned him off. I wrapped him in a blanket, put him in his car seat and drove home. My wife would kill me if she ever found out.

—ANONYMOUS
ST. LOUIS, MISSOURI
👶5 👶2

. . . .

I put cereal in their milk at about three months. That helped them sleep through the night.

—REBECCA JEAN GOINS
COLUMBUS, OHIO
👶33 👶20

The first year of life is the time of most rapid growth in our lives. Your baby's weight will triple and length will increase by one third during the first year. The brain (and head) will grow to 85 percent of adult size during this time. We never grow at such a rapid rate again!

MY FRIENDS AND FAMILY TOLD ME to just let my son cry, and to make sure he stayed on a four-hour eating schedule. But my son was hungry every three hours, so I had to put cereal in his formula at around three weeks old.

—TENESHA N. BENTON
STOCKBRIDGE, GEORGIA
👶6

. . . .

ONE MORNING, I AWOKE TO SCREAMS of delight coming from my 11-month-old daughter's room. As I rushed to greet her and whisk her out of her crib as usual, I was stopped by a dreadful sight: She had taken off her pajamas and her diaper, and had an artistic field day with her poop! She smeared it everywhere—on her teddy bear, her crib bedding, her mobile, herself. As a result, every night for the next year, I secured the zipper of her sleeper to the fabric with a diaper pin so she could never get to her diaper again. And I made sure she had plenty of crayons, markers and Play-Doh to satisfy her artistic bent.

—N.L.
ST. LOUIS, MISSOURI
👶19 👶17 👧22

. . . .

IF YOU'RE BREAST-FEEDING, start pumping as soon as you can and let your husband give the baby the last feeding of the day. Not only does it help him bond with the baby, it lets you go to bed earlier and get some rest before the middle-of-the-night feedings begin.

—BETH BROWN
CINCINNATI, OHIO
👶1

To be a good mother, you need your energy. If breast-feeding is depleting you of your strength, then just stop and use a bottle.

—ANONYMOUS
AUSTIN, TEXAS
👶3 👶1

Sleep? The ABCs of ZZZs

Most babies sleep a lot—at least we hope they do. New parents should take the opportunity to sleep while the baby sleeps. The sleep periods may be short, but anything is better than nothing. Many new moms think they should be doing chores while the baby sleeps. This is a productive idea only if she is not at all sleep-deprived. A better idea is to nap when the baby naps and get an answering machine to answer your phone. You can return the calls when you wake up. Sleeping when the baby sleeps is the key to healthy new parents, so it's surprising that it seems so hard for many moms to put into practice. Yes, it is hard to let some of the chores go, but laundry and dishes don't have feelings; enough rest can lead to greater enjoyment for the parents and their baby.

Another hint: take turns feeding the baby at night. Even if nursing, Dad can offer a bottle of pumped breast milk while Mom sleeps. (Many of the new breast pumps are great.) It gives a true sense of accomplishment for Dad and a few extra winks for Mom.

JUST GIVE UP THE NOTION THAT YOU WILL have a full night's sleep for years. It makes life easier—albeit more fatiguing.

—DICKIE
ATLANTA, GEORGIA
6M

* * * * * * * *

I GET ABOUT SIX HOURS A NIGHT (not all at one time). My daughter wakes up every two to two and half hours. On my husband's days off, I sleep all day. This really helps me get through the week. Before my baby was born, I slept 10 to 12 hours a night (no kidding!!) so this was a huge change!

—SARAH CROMWELL
RIVERBANK, CALIFORNIA
3M

* * * * * * * *

IF YOU HAVE PARENTS CLOSE BY, ask one of them to stay over when your baby is sick. My son had strep throat and he would not go to sleep and would not stop screaming. This went on for three nights in a row. On the third night, my mother came over and stayed up with him while I was able to sleep. You really need to reach out and ask for help; if you are tired, you are almost useless as a parent.

—ANONYMOUS
PACIFIC PALISADES, CALIFORNIA
3

WITH MY DAUGHTER, I LENGTHENED THE AMOUNT of time she slept at a stretch. During the day, I kept her awake longer and longer after nursing by playing with her and distracting her. Slowly she adjusted and slept for longer periods at night, too. By eight weeks, she slept through the night. I was so grateful!

—CHRISTY
ALLENTOWN, PENNSYLVANIA
👩 4 👩 2

The key is to marry someone who functions best when you don't. If you're both tired, you're going to kill each other. If you get rest, you'll sur-vive.

—D.M.
IOWA CITY,
IOWA
👩 16
👩 13

• • • • • • • •

I WISH I'D KNOWN THE EXTENT OF SLEEP deprivation that motherhood brings. My babies didn't sleep through the night until they stopped nursing, so I literally don't think I got a real night's sleep for three years or so.

—RACHEL LEON
CROTON-ON-HUDSON, NEW YORK
👩 5 👦 3

• • • • • • • •

WHEN MY KIDS WERE BABIES, I had my fair share of nights when they didn't want to go to sleep. Instead of driving them around in the car like most people do, I found it easier to take them for walks in their strollers. I think it was a combination of the cool evening air and the motion of the stroller, but they'd usually be asleep before we'd walked a couple of blocks.

—HELEN REICH
DUBOIS, PENNSYLVANIA
👦 43 👩 38 👦 33

FIGURE OUT WHAT WORKS FOR YOUR CHILD—and know that everyone is different. The only thing that worked to put my daughter to sleep was putting her in a sturdy backpack and walking around, until she fell asleep. For a time, it was the ONLY thing she'd sleep in.

—TINA SMITH
FORT COLLINS, COLORADO
👧4 👧2

• • • • • • • •

I just wish there was a way to stock up on sleep, create a reserve and use it after the baby comes.

—ADRIANE
FT. LAUDERDALE, FLORIDA
👧1

• • • • • • • •

MY OLDEST BOY DID NOT SLEEP for the first six months of his life unless he was on a warm body or somehow moving. In fact, for many weeks the only place he would sleep for more that an hour or so was a swing. I still vividly remember the panic surging through me when the batteries started to die in the middle of the night.

—EMILY
FREEPORT, MAINE
👦7 👦6

SWING SHIFT

FOR THE FIRST COUPLE MONTHS OF MY DAUGHTER'S LIFE, my wife and I followed a two nights on/two nights off parenting rotation, which was a lifesaver! One of us assumed complete responsibility for the baby's middle-of-the-night needs (changing, feeding, etc.), while the other slept in the guest room with a pillow over his/her head, and concentrated exclusively on getting a good night's sleep. It prevented burnout—48 hours is plenty of time to rejuvenate, and just enough to exhaust the other person.

—JORDAN GRAHAM
PARKER, COLORADO
8 1

. . . .

WITH OUR TWINS, EACH OF US WOULD TAKE ONE CHILD for a whole day. We would each feed, change, bathe, and wake up in the middle of the night for the child under our supervision for a full 24 hours. Then we would switch. This way, we could bond with each child and also keep track of diaper changes and feedings. And after our daughter started sleeping through the night at three months, we were each guaranteed a good night's rest every other night.

—M.A.
CONNECTICUT
- 3

TAKE TURNS DOING THE MIDNIGHT FEEDINGS so that each parent gets at least a night or two per week of nearly-full sleep. I worked outside the house, so my wife let me sleep during the week. In exchange I always took Friday and Saturday night. Not only did it help the wife and kids, I think it helped our marriage!

> —M.S.
> NEW YORK, NEW YORK
> 👶18 👶13

. . . .

MY HUSBAND AND I FIGURED OUT that if I fed the baby and then went to bed around 9:00 p.m. and he took the midnight feeding, we could each get a good stretch of sleep each night, which made all the difference for us.

> —MEGAN DEELEY
> LOVELAND, OHIO
> 👶7 👶5 👶3 👶1

. . . .

MY HUSBAND AND I SET UP a schedule where for four days during the week, I'd take the night shift, and then he'd take one night during the week and do Friday and Saturday nights. This way he could be well rested for work, and I could get a break on the weekends.

> —SUZANNE M. DONOVAN
> CINCINNATI, OHIO
> 👶1 👶4 👶3

TALK WITH YOUR SPOUSE about your middle-of-the-night plan before you go to sleep and even write down your promises. It's really hard in the middle of the night—when you're delirious and frustrated—to remember and stick to a plan. It helped us support each other when the baby screamed and cried.

—ANNE B.
SAN FRANCISCO, CALIFORNIA
👶1

. . . .

When it comes to getting a baby to sleep, what works for one won't necessarily work for another. You have to adapt.

—CHRISTINE MCCARTHY
PORT-ZELIENOPLE, PENNSYLVANIA
👶6 👶4 👶3 👶1.5

. . . .

DON'T SWEAT THE SMALL STUFF. When my sister's kids were young, they had to be in bed by seven p.m. If those kids weren't in bed by three minutes past seven, it was a major crisis. My motto is: Be sensible. If you get so upset about three minutes past bedtime, how on earth are you going to have any energy left when it really hits the fan?

—JERENE
WILLIAMSPORT, PENNSYLVANIA
👶13 👶12 👶-👶7

MY AUNT ALWAYS SAID TO REMEMBER that "once in a row is a habit." It's a saying I had in the back of my mind, nagging me whenever I did stupid things like picking up a crying 18-month-old at four a.m. and bringing him into bed with me. I knew he'd want to do it every time after that, but I figured getting more sleep was worth the possibility he'd want to get in bed with me every day. Of course, the four a.m. in-bed-with-Mommy kept up for two months! Most of the habits babies and toddlers become accustomed to—and which cause you grief—are the ones you create for them.

CHRISTINE BEIDEL
RUTHERFORD, NEW JERSEY
11 2

SLEEP TRAINING FALLS INTO TWO CAMPS: the CIO (cry it out) crowd and the AP (attachment parenting) crowd. Most parents I talked to said that CIO was the only thing that worked. Some struggled for years until they tried it. I thought for sure I was going to be AP, but after six months I had an experience that made me change my mind. He was crying in his crib, really wailing, and my husband and I rushed in and picked him up to see what was wrong. He immediately stopped crying and started smiling and laughing. That's when I knew I'd been had. I decided we should start sleep training and put him on a pretty strict sleeping schedule. It worked like a charm.

—BARBARA McGLAMERY

IT SOOTHES THE SOUL

DEVELOP A NAP-TIME ROUTINE. I read my kids a book, then they listen to music. That's how they fall asleep. We play stuff like Chicago and Neil Diamond for them through their entire nap-time. It works.

—FORREST
WELLINGTON, COLORADO
3 2

· · · · · · · · ·

CALMING CDs THAT BABIES AND GROWNUPS LOVE:
Waltz for Debby, Bill Evans
Kind of Blue, Miles Davis
Door Harp, Michael Houser
Solo Monk, Thelonius Monk

—KENNY F.
RED BOILING SPRINGS, TENNESSEE
3

· · · · · · · · ·

MUSIC WAS ONE OF THE KEY ELEMENTS to getting our baby to sleep. Soothing tunes were ones that contain no vocals—which seem to be distracting. For infants, try ones that also contain heartbeat sounds. My daughter, now four years old, still conks out when she listens to her favorite ragtime CD at bedtime.

—C. KARP
IRVINE, CALIFORNIA
4

IF YOU GET THEM ADDICTED TO SLEEPING with white noise tapes or music, that's the only way they'll be able to sleep. We made that mistake on our first baby. For our second kid, we just forced him to learn to fall asleep in silence, and once he got the hang of it, he was a much better sleeper than our daughter.

—M.S.
New York, New York
18 13

DON'T PUT THE BABY IN YOUR BED. The baby will get used to the warmth, the body contact. Get them used to sleeping in their own bed. We had a bassinet for our daughter right next to our bed. It kept her more comfortable, and she didn't wake up as much. It also helped us get sleep. If we heard a grunt, it was just a matter of looking over the bed rather than getting up.

—J.B.
EAST SYRACUSE, NEW YORK
2

. . . .

If you don't sleep when the baby's sleeping, you're sunk. Take naps.

—SHIRLEY GUTKOWSKI
SUN PRAIRIE, WISCONSIN
26 25 - 23 21

. . . .

YOU WILL FIND YOURSELF PROMISING your new child just about anything in the world if they will just go back to sleep after their middle-of-the-night feeding. By the middle of the second month, if my kid had been able to tally all the promises, I'd be out a fleet of new BMW's when he turns 16, a few motorcycles, a couple of all-expense-paid trips to Europe and Australia, and season passes to Disneyland every year.

—DAVE COHEN

THE BEST OF A BAD SITUATION

When our first was born, he used to cry those first few months because he was restless and couldn't sleep. Because my wife had the baby for the entire day, nighttime duties—including feedings—were my responsibility. I used to go into his room and just walk with him on my shoulder and hum, and while he would never fully sleep, he would calm down. Sometimes he would hum, too. The trick was that I knew this would be our routine every night, so I planned on it and looked forward to it, and I didn't try to rush back to bed.

Even though I got little sleep those first months, I found myself looking forward to the evening time I spent with my son. I told myself that no matter how much I wanted to be in bed, this was actually more enjoyable because it doesn't last, since they grow up so quickly. I was right. He's 14 now, and it seems like only yesterday he was a baby. I think of those evenings as fondly now as I felt when I was going through it.

—Tim O'Brien
Pittsburgh, Pennsylvania
14

ONE OF THE BIGGEST MISTAKES I made was having our baby sleep with us. She's now 16 months old and still sleeping with us. It's very hard to get them out of your bed once you get them in. I would love a good night's sleep; I haven't had one since she was born. If I ever have another child I will rent them their own apartment down the street.

> —J.V.
> LOS ANGELES, CALIFORNIA
> 🐾1

* * * * * * * *

IF YOU WAIT UNTIL YOUR BABY IS REALLY TIRED, he is actually overtired and will have a harder time falling asleep. Try to notice how your baby behaves right before he gets really tired and put him to sleep then, and he'll sleep better and longer.

> —K. JONES
> PHILADELPHIA, PENNSYLVANIA
> 🐾14 👶10 🐾6

* * * * * * * *

OUR BABY SLEPT THROUGH THE NIGHT after only three weeks! We made sure to only swaddle her at night and not have her take naps in her nighttime sleep area (crib) so that she knew the difference between night and day. She napped in the living room during the day.

> —ANONYMOUS
> ALAMEDA, CALIFORNIA
> 🐾7M

What's the secret to getting the kid back to sleep? I have no idea, since I can't really remember the first three months of his life.

—DAVE COHEN

DON'T LET YOUR BABY SLEEP WITH YOU, unless you really want to. We made the mistake of letting him sleep with us in the beginning. So at six months, we had to break him of the habit, which was hard. Luckily it only took a day or two, with a couple of hours of crying each night.

—BETHANY
FORT COLLINS, COLORADO
11M

· · · · · · · · ·

A LOT OF PEOPLE SAY NOT TO LET YOUR KIDS SLEEP in your bed, but I don't agree with that. We let our children sleep with us until they were two to three years old and it has made them more confident.

—ANNA EDELMAN
BROOKLYN, NEW YORK
7 2 7M

· · · · · · · · ·

THE WHOLE FAMILY IS BETTER OFF if you get some sleep. Sleep deprivation makes you act out of character. I would lose my temper. I would forget things. When my baby was six weeks old, I would hear him wake up, and I would just start crying.

—L.
CHARLOTTE, NORTH CAROLINA
2 1

When the baby cries in the middle of the night, don't argue about getting up. Just be glad you get to do it!

—MARK
NEW YORK,
NEW YORK

THE FATHER'S UNABRIDGED GUIDE TO AVOIDING CHILD CARE

New fathers will be shocked to learn that, even though they haven't been outfitted with mammaries, they will be fully expected to participate in the raising of an infant. Particularly horrifying is when the baby starts crying in the middle of the night, and the father is expected to get up and change diapers.

To get out of this duty, follow what I call the "W. Bruce Cameron Dictionary Method." Buy a thick hardcover dictionary of the English language, wrap it in towels, and place it in the baby's bedroom.

The next time the baby starts crying in the middle of the night, whisper sweetly to your wife, "Don't worry, honey, I'll take care of it." When you get to the baby's room, lift the dictionary above your head and drop it straight to the floor. This will make a loud bang that will resonate throughout every room of the house. Immediately afterward, scoop up your baby into your arms, and when your wife comes rushing in with a panicked look on her face, crying, "What just happened?" you can look back at her innocently and reply, "What do you mean? I didn't hear anything."

From this point forward, every time the baby cries in the middle of the night, she will insist on getting up to take care of it herself.

—W. Bruce Cameron
Santa Monica, California
22 20 16

SOME OF THE BEST ADVICE I got came from Harvey Karp's book *Best Baby on the Block*, in the chapter that describes how to swaddle your newborn. My husband named it the "baby burrito." We learned how to swaddle our son in a really tight burrito and it really worked—he slept like a champ! In fact, we continued to swaddle him for the first five months of his life. It has to be a really tight burrito—tighter than you would think. I couldn't find a blanket big enough in the store, so I bought material and had my mother-in-law sew the edges. It is a must!

—AMY
CINCINNATI, OHIO
👶3 👶1

• • • • • • • •

BABIES DO NOT BELONG IN THEIR PARENTS' BED under any circumstances. Even if you're not having sex, your bed has a feeling of intimacy associated with it, and adding a child to the equation ruins it.

—STEVEN GREEN
LOS ANGELES, CALIFORNIA
👪35 👶30 👶29 👶25 👶17

• • • • • • • •

A GOOD TIP TO HELP BABIES SLEEP is to make sure to turn off the lights when it is time to go to bed so they know the difference between daytime and bedtime. This helped my daughter develop a sleep pattern.

—TANYA ROCHELLE
SHERMAN OAKS, CALIFORNIA
👪1

My mom told me to sleep when the baby sleeps, and clean when he's awake. I took her advice, and was only half the zombie I would have been other-wise.

—A.B.
👪27
👪~👶23
👶21 👶10

LET SLEEPING BABIES SLEEP

One of the most important things to new parents (or any parent, really) is sleep. We discovered this in an unusual way when our daughter, Clara, was two days old. She wouldn't *stop* sleeping. She slept for over six straight hours, which seems like a long time when you are checking an infant's breathing every 15 minutes. This terrified me, I worried that she wasn't getting enough nutrition, as well as the fact that these hours of sleep were all during the day. I called my mother, who said, "Never wake a sleeping baby." I called my friend Michelle, who said, "Never wake a sleeping baby." I called the La Leche League, and they said, "Wake the infant every two hours to nurse all day and all night." I called the advice line at the pediatrician's office, and they said, "Wake the baby every two hours to nurse only during the day." I stopped calling people. Clara slept through the night on day three, and I learned the true joy of a full night's sleep.

—KATHERINE
OAKLAND, CALIFORNIA
2

SHOULD OUR BABY SLEEP IN OUR BED?

Current recommendations vary, but I suggest that as long as the baby is still nursing at night, she should be close by (usually in a cradle, bassinet, or crib in your bedroom.) This makes nursing more convenient; The mother can get up and nurse the baby sitting in a convenient chair, or even in her bed. It often happens that a nursing mother will sometimes fall asleep during a night feeding. Usually, that's fine, but it is a good idea to return the baby to her sleeping spot after nursing. As previously mentioned, it is also a wonderful thing for fathers to take responsibility for at least one nighttime feeding by using pumped breast milk in a bottle, or formula if the baby is bottle fed. Remember, though, that breast milk is always available and at the right temperature. Bottle feeding takes a bit more preparation.

OUR FIRST BIG MISTAKE WITH OUR FIRST CHILD was to not be regimented enough about sleep. We didn't create any kind of solid schedule, and our daughter's sleep habits suffered because of it. Today, she's 11 and still doesn't sleep well. We learned to get tougher with our other kids, and it made a huge difference for them. Be sure to set a disciplined sleep schedule. Even if it seems mean, you're doing everyone a favor in the long run.

—HILLARY
MADEIRA, OHIO
😊8 😊-😊3 👧11

• • • • • • • •

WHEN MY TWINS SLEPT TOGETHER, they always had to sleep with their foreheads touching, and it was so sweet! No matter where they started out the night or the nap, they always ended up sleeping forehead-to-forehead.

—MANDY PARROT
LOVELAND, OHIO
👧5 😊-👧1

• • • • • • • •

MY HUSBAND AND I HAD WANTED my son to start sleeping in his own bed. My grandmother had me put a shirt that had my scent on it in the crib with him so he could just assume that I was around—and it worked. I did that for about a week. After that, he got used to sleeping in his bed.

—MELANIE WILLIAMS
ATLANTA, GEORGIA
😊 4

My husband and I would take turns sleeping in on the weekends—one day each—so we could catch up.

— MARY WALSH
CINCINNATI,
OHIO
😊 6 😊 4
😊 1 👧 7

SLEEP NOT

I LIVE IN A ONE-BEDROOM APARTMENT. Until my daughter was four months old, we were all able to sleep pretty well. Then she suddenly stopped sleeping. She would sleep while my husband and I were in the living room, but as soon as we got into our bed, she would wake up and start screaming. We eventually bought a divider and sectioned off a space in the living room just for her, and everyone is sleeping tight.

—DANIELLE
ORANGE, CALIFORNIA

ONE NIGHT, WHEN MY DAUGHTER was about three months old and I had just gone back to work, I put her down at about 9:00 and she woke up at 10:00, 11:00, and 12:00, and then every hour on the hour. There was nothing I could do to get her to stop screaming. I tried feeding her, holding her, patting her, and sleeping with her in my bed. Eventually, I started crying. I knew what was in store for me at work the next day and I was getting no sleep.

—MARLA
BURBANK, CALIFORNIA

ONCE I ACCEPTED THAT IT WOULD BE a very long time before
I would sleep through the night, it made it much easier.

—SUZANNE NAYDUCH
FORT COLLINS, COLORADO
8M

* * * * * * * *

EXERCISE AND A BABY'S NAPTIME really can go together. I
always opted for a stationary bike or the treadmill, with
its low and steady rumbling and light vibrations in the
floor to make my baby sleep. Put the baby's bassinet
next to the stationary bike, start pedaling away, make
eyes at the child, and he or she will be asleep in no time.

—TED RINEY
DALLAS, TEXAS

* * * * * * * *

OUR DAUGHTER SPENT NINE DAYS in the NICU after she
was born, and we were used to her easily falling asleep
at the end of each feeding. But once we got her home,
she seemed to take forever to fall asleep. When we finally
did get her to sleep, she was often awake again an hour
and a half later. I was miserable and my husband was
just trying to keep me calm; he now says that the worst
moments were when I was pounding my head against the
mattress in frustration.

—ELIZABETH
GAINESVILLE, FLORIDA
1

Put the
bassinet in
the living
room with
you while
you're
watching TV.
It teaches
the baby to
sleep
through a
lot of noise.

—ANONYMOUS
WASHINGTON,
DC
12

AT AROUND FOUR MONTHS, start putting the baby down when he's awake and let him learn how to fall asleep on his own. It was hard at first, and they do cry, but it was worth it. Once they got that down, bedtime was so much easier, and they could get themselves back to sleep in the middle of the night, so we didn't have to!

—MEGAN DEELEY
LOVELAND, OHIO
7 5 3 1

It's never too early to start a bed-time routine. It will help them go to sleep better right away, and espe-cially down the road.

—*A.L.*
BOSTON,
MASSACHUSETTS
6 4

ONE NIGHT MY DAUGHTER was up every fifteen minutes, screaming with gas pain. I didn't know what to do to help her. I was so tired that I just broke down and cried. During those moments it is hard to see the light at the end of the tunnel, but it's there, so you have to do your best to hold on and keep it together.

—LILY
DIX HILLS, NEW YORK
1

WHEN MY BABY WAS BORN, I started lying to my wife for the first time. The baby never slept at night for the first couple of months. Sometimes when I got off work, I was so tired I told my wife I was going to help my brother with some stuff around his house; I was really going over there to sleep. I know it was wrong, but I don't feel bad.

—SEAN
JOLIET, ILLINOIS
15 13 1

THREE Z'S FOR FERBER

My youngest was a terrible sleeper. I read every book I could get my hands on and talked to lots of other parents. Nothing worked. Everyone in our household, especially my nine month-old baby, was completely exhausted from waking repeatedly every night and completely stressed from the bedtime "ritual" which could literally go on for hours. I decided to try the Ferber method, basically letting him cry. I had tremendous guilt about trying this method. I think it took about a week. It was very stressful—I cried and screamed at my husband if he was even a minute late going in to comfort the baby when it was his turn. But, lo and behold, my baby became a terrific sleeper! He is now two years old and is a very happy, very energetic, very bright child who loves his bedtime routine, goes to sleep usually without a fuss, and takes three-hour naps. I am just amazed now when he trots off down the hall with his dad at bedtime and says "Night-night, Mom, I love you." Now I feel guilty about not doing what needed to be done sooner so that the poor little guy could get some sleep!

—ANONYMOUS
DALLAS, TEXAS
3 2

MY SON WOULD NEVER SLEEP during the day. I tried holding him in a sling, and putting him in a bouncy seat, but nothing worked. After four days in a row when I didn't even get to take a shower, my husband came home from work one night and told me I smelled. He forced me to get in the shower, and the next day he came home with a battery-operated baby swing. It saved my life.

—JILLIAN
TEMPE, ARIZONA
👶1

. . . .

WE USE A SOUND MACHINE in our son's room when it's time for him to sleep. The white noise helps him fall asleep, and it muffles the sounds of traffic or the neighbors' kids playing outside.

—BETH BROWN
CINCINNATI, OHIO
👶1

. . . .

MY HUSBAND AND I WORKED OUT a system that helped us get as much sleep as we could. I would get up with the baby in the middle of the night, and he would take the wake-up shift first thing in the morning. He had to get up then for work anyway, so at least we could each get a good stretch of sleep every night, and I could sleep a little later in the morning after he left for work.

—SHERRY
SOUTH LEBANON, OHIO
👶6 👶4 👶1

> *The best night of sleep I ever had was when my mom came to visit. I actually slept: that was fantastic.*
>
> —CANDACE NICHELLE BRUMFIELD WEST PALM BEACH, FLORIDA
> 👶7 👶4 👶1

SLEEP REQUIREMENTS

Babies need different amounts of sleep depending on their age, size, and growth spurts. Newborns may sleep up to 20 hours a day, with interruptions only to eat, pee, and poop (and sometimes the latter two occur during sleep.) If your baby suddenly seems to want to eat more and sleep more, it is probably because he is undergoing a period of rapid growth. Most sleep periods occur when the baby is full and relaxed (often after a good feeding or a bath). Unless your pediatrician tells you differently, let your baby sleep as long as he wants to, wait until he is fully awake, and then feed him. Bowel movements often follow a good feeding, so it's not a bad idea to plan to change diapers after a good nursing or bottle feed.

FOR A WHILE WHEN MY SON was about five months old he would not go to bed without crying. There were times I was up with him all night. When I was on maternity leave, it was fine, but once I went back to work it was unbearable. I was ready to check myself into a mental hospital. One night I decided to give him a bath right before bed and within minutes of putting him down, he was fast asleep. I started giving him baths every night right before bed and except for the nights when he's been sick, he hasn't cried once.

—ANONYMOUS
LOS ANGELES, CALIFORNIA
2

My baby was a two-hour baby. He slept two hours and was up two hours.

—RENEE
CHICAGO,
ILLINOIS
29

ALWAYS GET UP BEFORE YOUR CHILD WAKES, whether to read the paper and have coffee, do yoga, meditate. If you don't have some alone time in the morning, your day is spent playing catch-up. As soon as I hear a bird chirp, I think, "Grab this moment!"

—P. SUPPIGER
OAKLAND, CALIFORNIA
5   2

CHAPTER

Crying: It Can Drive You to Tears

You communicate with your baby with a soft gentle voice, loving words, smiling, touching, and stroking. Your baby, especially during the early months, communicates by crying and fussing. Later this will develop into grunting, cooing, and smiling. There are many reasons that babies cry, and as time goes by you will learn to interpret different cries as hunger, discomfort, or the need of a diaper change. There are times, though, when your baby will cry for no apparent reason. You have changed the diaper; swaddled the baby (meaning, you wrapped him up tightly in a receiving blanket);

rocked, cuddled, and spoken to your baby without any decrease in crying. You don't know what else to try.

I like to think of these times as baby exercise. Your baby has only a few ways to exercise and increase his heart rate, breathing rate, and muscle tone; crying is one of them. If you are convinced your baby is fine in every way, sometimes the best thing to do is to do nothing. Wrap the baby up (or not) and return him to a safe place (crib, bassinet, cradle, play pen, etc) and let the crying continue.

Remember that babies can sense and respond to caregiver stress. If you are upset about something, try to calm yourself down before trying to calm your baby. If you have a backup caregiver available (the other parent, a friend, relative, or neighbor), ask for help. Turn the crying baby over to someone you trust and have a quiet period for yourself. Even a brief period of rest or a short nap works wonders in these situations.

A BABY CAN SENSE WHEN YOU'RE STRESSED. You have to stay calm, even if your heart is in your throat. Try to soothe instead of getting involved in the hysteria your baby is involved in. The more stressed you get, the more it rubs off on your baby.

> —J.B.H.
> ALEXANDRIA, VIRGINIA
> 🐣 3M

• • • • • • • •

WHEN YOUR NEWBORN CRIES A LOT and you're at the end of your rope, just put them in their crib, shut the door and come back in 15 minutes to try again after you've collected yourself. That's what I always did and it saved me a lot of stress.

> —KRISTI
> CEDAR RAPIDS, IOWA
> 👶 2

• • • • • • • •

MY DAUGHTER SCREAMED FOR THE ENTIRE first year. I just tried to keep from jumping out the window. I held her incessantly and breastfed her incessantly and tried to pay attention to her as much as possible. That first year was very tough— she was not a cute baby. She was not fun.

> —DEB S.
> EL CAJON, CALIFORNIA
> 🐣 22 👶 13

Remember, this, too, will pass. Remind yourself that things are not always going to be this way.

—W.F.
MERTZTOWN,
PENNSYLVANIA
🐣 24 👶 20

IF THE BABY IS GOING CRAZY CRYING, step out of the room, take some deep breaths, and then come back. You need to get yourself together, no matter what's happening with the child.

—SHANI WERHLE
ISRAEL

• • • • • • • •

Babies don't die from crying. But they do learn from it. If you jump to respond to crying, they'll expect you to come running every time they do it.

—CATHY
ST. LOUIS PARK, MINNESOTA
11 7

• • • • • • • •

WHEN IT COMES TO GETTING BABIES TO STOP crying you really have to be creative. When my daughter would cry and cry for no reason, we found that giving her an ice cube to play with and suck on a little really calmed her. Bizarre but true.

—ROB MARINO
EAST LIVERPOOL, OHIO
19 14

MELTDOWN IN AISLE 9

KEYS AND TIC-TACS ARE GOOD DEVICES FOR SOOTHING a crying baby in the supermarket. They're like little rattles. And if your baby is old enough, sit them up on the counter or the little shelf where you sign your credit card receipts— it usually surprises them so much they stop crying.

—DAN DUPONT
ARLINGTON, VIRGINIA
6 3 3M

KEEP THEM MOVING AND THEY'RE USUALLY FINE. Pick them up and rock them—it's easy enough to push the cart with your stomach if you're already in line. Or leave enough space between you and the person in front of you to rock the cart back and forth.

—JAY JOHNSON
LANSING, MICHIGAN
13 11 8 20M

IF YOUR BABY IS CRYING ON LINE AT THE SUPERMARKET, look for someone who loves kids to distract him.

—STEVEN SHELTON
WICHITA FALLS, TEXAS
30 22

WHEN OUR DAUGHTER CRIED, we made sure nothing was seriously wrong, and then we'd put her in her bouncy chair, the crib, or the Pack-n-Play, and let her cry. Usually, she would calm herself down. But before we put her down, we would always hug her and tell her we loved her.

—ANONYMOUS
LIVERPOOL, NEW YORK
👶10 👧8

A calm temperament helps, but if you don't have one you're not going to suddenly develop one when your baby is crying.

—BARBARA STEWART
SEATTLE, WASHINGTON
👶20 👧17

I USED TO PRETEND THAT A HIDDEN CAMERA was in the room with me and that I had to keep my cool in case they showed it on "Oprah" or something. It forced me say to myself, "Would I want other people to see how I am reacting right now?"

—WENDY SNYDER
WESTMINSTER, COLORADO
👧8 👧4

THERE WERE TIMES WHEN MY BABY would do nothing but scream and cry. I went berserk trying to figure out why. She was cleaned, fed and not hot or cold. Then my mother said, "Well, maybe she is teething." Sure enough, after I gave her teething balm, she stopped crying.

> —DAWN COLCLASURE-WILSON
> RANCHO MIRAGE, CALIFORNIA
> 2

*One word:
Earplugs.*

—JOHN RODGERS
SEATTLE,
WASHINGTON
9

IF YOU CAN REMEMBER THAT BABIES are simply communicating the best way they can when they cry, you may be able to find the humor in it all. I think babies are so adorable when they make that crying face! So I laugh and it keeps my mood elevated and patient while I wait out the crying.

> —MONICA AND TODD DENNIS
> BRIDGEPORT, CONNECTICUT
> 4   6M

MY HUSBAND AND I FOUND ONLY TWO THINGS that worked to stop my daughter from crying. One was to put her in her car seat and drive around. The other was to take her into the laundry room, and turn the clothes dryer on. The heat combined with the humming sound calmed her down.

> —SANDI
> ALLENTOWN, PENNSYLVANIA
> 11

THE GREAT PACIFIER DEBATE

DON'T USE PACIFIERS. First off, a little crying never hurt a child. Second, pacifiers are not good for the gums and teeth.

—JEANNE ECKMAN
LANCASTER, PENNSYLVANIA
11 -5

• • • • • • • • •

YOU ARE NOT "PLUGGING UP THE BABY" by using a pacifier. The ones made today are shaped so that they don't cause dental problems.

—KATHY PENTON
SAVANNAH, GEORGIA
23

• • • • • • • • •

IT WAS COMICAL THAT A LITTLE PIECE OF PLASTIC and rubber controlled not only my daughter but me, too. One time, I took the kids sightseeing to an old military fort. When it was time to leave, the kids were tired and my daughter started crying. I tore that van apart but no pacifier! I couldn't face a 30-minute drive with her screaming the whole way, so I packed everyone up and drove straight to the store to buy two pacifiers—one to give her, and one to store in the van.

—JOHN D'EREDITA
SYRACUSE, NEW YORK
19 12

WE DIDN'T WANT TO USE A PACIFIER, but it only took one week of crying for us to give in. From the minute we put it in, he was happy. I prefer the pacifier over the thumb—we can always take the pacifier away.

— KRISTIN KELLEY
ANNANDALE, VIRGINIA
2

• • • • • • • • •

I OFFERED A PACIFIER TO EACH BABY because I figured it would be an easier habit to break than a thumb. But guess what? That is really the baby's decision. All three of mine absolutely refused to use a pacifier.

—HEIDE A.W. KAMINSKI
TECUMSEH, MICHIGAN
18   15   6

• • • • • • • • •

MY SON WAS THOROUGHLY ADDICTED to his pacifier. To wean him off of it, we told him that when he turned three he would be too old for his pacifier, and because of this, it would break. The night before my son's third birthday my husband and I went around the house cutting off the tips of all the pacifiers. In the morning, my son ran up to me crying, "Mommy, Mommy! You were right! I'm three today and my pacifier is broken!" That was it. He never asked for it again.

—PAMELA BARTH
BAKERSFIELD, CALIFORNIA
20   17   3   9M

THE FIRST NIGHT WE TOOK MY SON'S PACIFIER AWAY there was no argument or even crying. The next night we had 45 minutes of screaming and smashing the crib against the wall. The third night went without incident and he's been happily "binky"-free ever since.

—CHRISTINE BEIDEL
RUTHERFORD, NEW JERSEY
11 2

• • • • • • • • •

THE CONVENTIONAL WISDOM about pacifiers and breast-feeding is that you are a bad mother if you use a pacifier and if you don't breast-feed. There is nothing wrong with a pacifier. It helps to soothe your baby while you hold her or let her sit in a swing. Don't be afraid to let your newborn spend a little time out of your loving arms. And don't feel guilty for wanting to sleep. I tried for a few weeks to breast-feed, but if I had relied solely on that, my daughter would have starved. It just works better for some women than others. As long as your baby is fat and happy with a smile on her face, you are probably doing just fine.

—ANONYMOUS
FT. LEE, NEW JERSEY
2

WHEN YOUR BABY CRIES, rather than getting frustrated, join the chorus. Sometimes Junior really appreciates the crooning company.

—DICKIE
ATLANTA, GEORGIA
6M

* * * * * * * *

Get away from the crying for a moment—even if you just go stand in the shower. Know your limits and know when to ask for help. Moms have to take care of themselves, too.

—J.R.
CHICAGO, ILLINOIS
21 18

* * * * * * * *

THIS RUNS CONTRARY TO THE ADVICE my parents gave me, but I believe very strongly if your baby is crying, pick her up. Don't let her cry it out. Babies' wants are their needs. I don't think it's possible to spoil a baby—a toddler, yes, but not a baby.

—MARY BRIGHT
ALLENTOWN, PENNSYLVANIA
33 31

CRY LIKE A BABY

Crying is normal; it's one of the ways a newborn communicates. As you and your newborn get to know each other better you will be able to identify what each cry means. (Moms often figure this out before dads.) At first, however, crying can make new parents feel either anxious or utterly miserable. It helps to be prepared; a good way to do that is to have a list of the possible reasons for crying. In this way, you have a better chance of managing the crying and staying calm. The list in order of importance might be something like this:

- Is the baby hungry?
- Is the diaper wet or full?
- Does the baby have gas and need additional burping for relief?
- Could the clothing or diaper be too tight?
- Is the baby too hot or cold?
- Is the baby tired?
- Is the baby's temperature elevated?

Babies also respond to stressed parents and care-givers with their own stress, expressed as crying. Take a few deep breaths and calm yourself first before trying to calm your baby.

Sometimes, however, you run through your entire list twice and the baby is still crying. If you have done every-thing you can think of and nothing has worked, the baby might just need to cry. Some babies cry for exercise. Think of it as baby jogging, leave him or her in a safe place like a crib or play pen, and take a time-out yourself.

ROCK, NURSE, DANCE, WEAR A SLING, DRIVE in the car, administer gripe water and Simethicone drops. Different strategies work for different kids. Our son liked to be jogged around the room to music—particularly loud industrial music. He liked Ministry and Nine Inch Nails. And so do I.

—MARRIT INGMAN
AUSTIN, TEXAS
2

Letting my son 'cry it out' was one of the most triumphant decisions I've made as a parent. It proved my theory that if you stop rewarding bad behavior, the behavior stops.

—SARAH
ST. LOUIS PARK, MINNESOTA
5

MY DAUGHTER'S FIRST FEW WEEKS AT HOME, she would cry all the time. If it got unbearable, I would have to let my husband take over, or walk away for a few minutes. A screaming baby really does take its toll on the nerves.

—MARIA FERRANTI
TORONTO, ONTARIO, CANADA
7M

CURING WHAT AILS YOU

When my daughter was a baby, my husband and I rocked her to sleep each night. It was a special time, but often when we tried to sneak her into her crib after she had fallen asleep, she would wake up again, screaming. So then we'd have to rock her to sleep again.

When she was a year old, I spoke with a pediatrician, who said we had to stop doing this, for our good and for hers. He said no matter how hard it was, we needed to put her in her crib and just let her cry.

The first night we did it, our daughter cried for a half hour. I cried too, as my husband and I sat downstairs and listened. But we didn't go to her. It was amazing: The second night she cried only for five minutes, and the third night she didn't cry at all. After a year of having such a hard time getting her to sleep, our daughter was "cured" in three nights!

—SANDI
ALLENTOWN, PENNSYLVANIA
11

TEETHING WISDOM

IF YOUR BABY IS TEETHING and keeping the whole family up at night crying because of it, rub a little (just a little) whiskey on his or her gums to numb the pain. It works wonders. You might want to rub a little on your own gums as well.

—JILL FULLEN
SWISSVALE, PENNSYLVANIA
👶24

. . . .

ONE TIME, WHEN OUR SON WAS TEETHING, we put him in a stroller and wheeled him around the house. As long as we moved, he was fine. As soon as we stopped, he'd cry again. Everyone took turns wheeling him around. We have a really cute video of our baby with his grandpa walking behind him, and the dog walking behind them. It was a parade!

—LINDA BOWER
LOVELAND, COLORADO
👶9 🐕6

. . . .

I SOAKED A CLEAN TOWEL IN APPLE JUICE and froze it. It seemed to soothe him immediately. I got the idea from my dog trainer, who once told me to put peanut butter on a towel, soak it in water, and freeze it to use as a toy.

—DANI
HOLLYWOOD, FLORIDA
👶2

OUR SON LOVES TO CHEW on a wet face cloth that's been in the freezer for about an hour.

—BETH BROWN
CINCINNATI, OHIO

WHEN MY DAUGHTER WAS TEETHING I gave her a big frozen banana to suck and chew on.

—ANONYMOUS
MOBILE, ALABAMA

WHEN MY DAUGHTER WAS TEETHING, I gave her frozen bagels to suck and chew on. This way she was able to soothe her gums and have a yummy snack at the same time.

—ANONYMOUS
DALLAS, TEXAS

FOR TEETHING, I dipped a cloth in breast milk and then froze it.

—ANONYMOUS
HOLLYWOOD, FLORIDA

WHEN SHE CRIES AND THE REASON IS NOT OBVIOUS (she's not hungry, wet, tired, or sick), standing up and holding her while you bounce from one foot to another works 90 percent of the time.

—ANONYMOUS
ALAMEDA, CALIFORNIA
7M

• • • • • • • • •

AFTER A COUPLE OF WEEKS of nightly crying, with me trying everything from feeding to burping to rocking, I realized that the baby was just tired and everything I was doing to help her was actually making it worse. When I started putting her in her bassinet and just letting her fuss a little, she would fall asleep within five minutes. She was then consistently asleep by nine p.m. and could fall asleep on her own without crying at all.

—SHAUNA FARRELL
VANCOUVER, BC, CANADA
2 8M

• • • • • • • • •

WE SING AND DANCE WITH HER. We make the baby happy, we bounce her around a bit, and we move her legs like she's J. Lo— well, maybe her moves aren't as smooth, but once she's moving, she's happy.

—ELIZABETH GIARMUNDEA

For crying babies, be sure to check everything— teething, hunger, dirty diaper—then, resort to vacuuming, driving, or the swing. Music helps too.

—E. HIRSH
WEST PALM
BEACH, FLORIDA
7

WHEN YOUR BABY IS CRYING and they stop for a moment to see if they can hear you coming, it's probably not that bad. They are just learning the fine points of manipulating their environment (and conditioning you at the same time).

—R.A.
CEDAR RAPIDS, IOWA
24 22

. . . .

I USED TO HOLD MY SON AND DANCE HIM all around the room, singing either to music on the radio, or to songs I had stored in my head. (One night I sang all the Herman's Hermits songs I could remember, which turned out to be a surprising amount!) We'd dance for hours at a time. I really miss those days.

—STEPHANIE WOLFE
GROTON, CONNECTICUT
23M

. . . .

SOMETIMES, IT'S OK TO LET A BABY CRY. Babies have to exercise their lungs sometimes. With my oldest son, it was simple. I'd put him in his bed, check if he was hungry, check for a tummy ache, and so on. If he kept crying, I shut the door, I let him cry and I didn't let it bother me.

—THOMAS M.W. "MIKE" DOWNS
SYRACUSE, NEW YORK
20 16 13 10

Don't listen to the old wives' tales about how holding your baby too much spoils them. It doesn't spoil them. It makes them feel loved and babies need to feel loved.

— GUADALUPE
GOMEZ
AZUSA,
CALIFORNIA
36 34
31

YOU MUST LEARN YOUR BABY'S CRIES. My first son had a squeaky cry, which meant he wanted to get picked up. He also had a sniffling cry, which meant he was wet. A low, whining cry meant he was sleepy. When I heard that cry, I knew there would be silence in about ten minutes. But the cry that was most important was his cry of hunger. This cry was a loud, angry cry, as if someone has just given him a shot. It took me nearly three months to learn it, but I listened intently, and knowing it came in handy.

—BEATRICE CHAPPELL
CHICAGO, ILLINOIS
26 19 18

To stop our babies from crying, my husband would place the baby across his lap, face down, and give the kid a back rub. Worked almost every time.

—V.B.
DOHA, QATAR
23
21 14

• • • • • • • • •

I SPEND A LOT OF TIME WALKING with my son around the house to keep him from crying. Sometimes, though, I have to set him down and walk outside for five minutes just so I do not have to keep listening. That little break helps a lot.

—MICHELLE M.
OOSTBURG, WISCONSIN
2 2M

• • • • • • • • •

I HAVE FOUND THAT WHEN NOTHING ELSE will work, get out the Tylenol. If you are against that, then try sleeping upright with the baby on you in a recliner. That helps sometimes.

—TONYA LEE
MOUNT AIRY, MARYLAND
8 5

TO SOOTHE OUR CHILDREN IN THEIR CRIBS, we found a vibrating attachment at Wal-Mart that clipped on to a crib or bassinet. Switching it on created a gentle movement that soothed the children— especially when they were tired.

—ELAINE MCGUIRE
WINDSOR, COLORADO
😊20 😊18 😊6 😊4

* * * * * * * *

FOR A WHILE, THE ONLY THING that would make my daughter stop crying was the vibrating chair. One night, when I put her in it, it stopped vibrating. She started screaming her head off. It was after nine at night, so I couldn't go to the store to buy a new one. My husband ended up walking down the block asking our neighbors if they had one we could borrow. He ended up knocking on six doors before he found one. If you have a piece of equipment that you depend on, have an extra one on hand.

—ANONYMOUS
SANTA MONICA, CALIFORNIA
😊2

* * * * * * * *

WHEN THE MOM OR DAD IS STRESSED OUT from the newborn's crying, have the other parent take the baby out on a walk, either in a carrier or a stroller. Even if it doesn't settle the baby, it gives the stressed-out parent a break.

—AMY
CINCINNATI, OHIO
😊3 😊1

A GREAT TIME TO TAKE A SHOWER is just after you put the baby to bed—and the baby's still crying. Not only will this prevent you from running to pick up the baby when what he really needs is sleep, it's doubly relaxing because: a) it's a hot shower, and b) you can't hear the crying.

—HEIDI
CHICAGO, ILLINOIS
😊14 😊11 🐵6

• • • • • • • • •

THE HARDEST PART OF THE FIRST THREE MONTHS was that 4:00 p.m. fussy time, when the baby would cry nonstop. Try to plan something to do every day at that time to help you get through it, even if it's just getting outside for a walk. A change of environment works wonders for both you and the baby.

—JULI KEDROWSKI
MAINEVILLE, OHIO
😊4 🐵6

When you feel the anger and frustration building up inside you, walk away.

—DAVID
DENVER,
COLORADO
😊11
🐵-😊4

Relativity: Parents, Grandparents & Everyone

As a new parent, you will receive parenting advice from many sources, including friends, relatives, and neighbors. It is important to listen to this advice, thank the advisor, and use whatever information you feel is valuable. Many books, magazines, and articles are available to help you become a better parent, but ultimately the decisions are yours. Take verbal advice graciously and use whatever part of it fits into your parenting style. Grandparents are a special source of information because of their unique bond to you and to your children. They always want what is best for you and your baby, but remember, it may have been a very long time since they dealt with an infant, memory can do strange things over the decades.

When you have important questions about raising your baby, your pediatrician (or the practice's advice nurse) will often be your most reliable source of information.

DON'T BE FOOLED BY ALL THE PEOPLE who paint parent-hood as this rosy, soft-focus thing. It's hard every single day. There are days during the first few weeks of parent-hood where the baby does nothing but cry and eat and poop, and you'll be tired and cranky and you'll wish you had never gotten pregnant. And that's OK. You aren't evil if you sometimes regret this huge thing that happened. Those thoughts are usually fleeting. And it does get bet-ter and easier over time.

—R.
REDMOND, WASHINGTON
6

Take a shower before your husband goes to work.

—L.G.
WEST NEW YORK, NEW JERSEY
2

• • • • • • • • •

MY HUSBAND IS A GREAT DAD and picks up a lot of the slack, but it's still hard. I think he wants to live in a sitcom from the '50s where after a long day he comes home to a perfect house with a perfect wife and perfect kids. That's never going to happen, but hopefully when I get more used to having both kids all the time he can at least come home to a house that's not a complete disaster, a wife that's not pulling her hair out, and two children that are wonderful, even though they're not perfect.

—SARAH SISSON CHRISTENSEN
SAN DIEGO, CALIFORNIA
2 2M

AFTER YOUR WIFE HAS A BABY, be home with her more. Wake up in the middle of the night and help. Some men run away. But I think you need to share. It's not just her child; it's yours, too.

—BATIA ELKAYAM
LOS ANGELES, CALIFORNIA

When you have your first baby, it is a monumental change in life. You go through a period of mourning/grief for the old life that is lost, and never to be known again. Life will never be the same as it was before.

—SHER JOHNSON
EL SEGUNDO, CALIFORNIA
11 8 5.5M

IF YOU ARE BOTTLE-FEEDING, I suggest dads feed the baby at least once a day. That will help them bond, as well as help mom.

—SHARI LEE SUGARMAN
NORTH BABYLON, NEW YORK
9W

IN YOUR DREAMS

There's nothing more exciting than being pregnant for the first time. You can visualize exactly how it will be—your angelic little baby smiling up at you, happily breast-feeding. You know the rules you'll set—no videos, no pacifier, no artificial colors or flavors, maybe you'll even cultivate a garden and only feed your baby foods that come from your own pesticide-free soil. Yet here you are, six months later, in line at Target buying Gerber's turkey-ham surprise and Barney videos, while your baby is propped in the stroller happily alternating between its pacifier and bottle.

Don't let others define for you what makes a "perfect" mom. A "perfect" mom listens and responds to the needs of both her child and herself. A perfect mom is the mom who allows a pacifier if that's what will soothe the baby; who pops open the jar of Gerber's or can of formula if that's what will make it easier and therefore less stressful for her; who sets up the playpen in front of a video for five minutes so she can take a shower.

—ANDREA MENSCHEL
CALABASAS, CALIFORNIA
8 5

I FEEL LIKE I TOOK A HUGE STEP in being a woman when I had a baby. When other mothers looked at me, it was like they were saying, "Welcome to the club!" I feel a strong connection to my mother as well as other mothers because of it.

—LESLIE BUNDY
WAUKESHA, WISCONSIN
1

*What sur-
prised me is
how the
baby comes
first.
Always.
Every time.*

*—M.S.L.
WAIKOLOA,
HAWAII
40 37*

MY HUSBAND IS SUCH A COMPETENT, confident person that not knowing exactly what to do with our baby was unfamiliar territory for him. After quite a few arguments, I realized that it's critical to make a father feel competent. Encourage and support him with his baby and give him lots of opportunities to succeed. For example, in the beginning let him hold the baby at times when the baby's likely to be calm.

—ROBYN
BIGLERVILLE, PENNSYLVANIA
1

FIRST-TIME MOTHERHOOD IS A 24/7 learning experience, but the most important thing I can say is to trust your instincts. You won't realize how much you really know about being a mother until you're going through it, and then you'll see: Women are made to be mothers.

—SUSAN MAROSITZ
CLIFTON, NEW JERSEY
19M

I'M IN A DINNER CLUB WITH A GROUP of women. We run the gamut—professional women, a 39-year-old friend who was recently engaged, a few moms who work, some who don't. There's a sense that we all want to be able to quote the front page of the Wall Street Journal, prepare a gourmet dinner for our family after a day in court, plan our child's birthday party, and watch their gymnastics class . . . but you can't do it all.

—MARYBETH
SAN FRANCISCO, CALIFORNIA
4

> *Don't judge your husband too harshly.*
>
> —ANONYMOUS
> LIVERPOOL,
> NEW YORK
> 7 5

. . . .

HERE'S A PIECE OF ADVICE that many mothers receive, but few follow: Take time for yourself. Babies are sweet, cute, cuddly, and very demanding. All the time. As they grow into toddlers, they are still sweet, cute, cuddly, and even more demanding. All the time. When I say to take time for yourself, I mean to go away for at least one week every year. Go someplace where you can relax and take care of yourself. Don't feel guilty. Leave the child with your husband and/or parents. They'll be fine. And you'll be even better when you return. (Start planning next year's trip shortly after you return!)

—E.G.
NEW HAVEN, CONNECTICUT
20

BABY BLUES

DEVELOP POSTPARTUM RITUALS. Every day for a month after I gave birth to twins I broke down in tears at four p.m. At first it wore us out. Then, one day, my husband noticed I was about to hit that low and he said, "Are you about to have high tea?" After that, every day when I felt "high tea" coming on he sat me down in the same living room chair and brought me a beer and a box of Kleenex. I cried, sipped my beer, and sat. Knowing we had developed this ritual together made my "high tea" something that I did not dread or fear.

—S.
PORTLAND, MAINE

FOR THE "BABY BLUES," GO TO ACUPUNCTURE—it gets everything aligned. Acupuncture in general helps to relax and balance energy, which often is enough to ease depression.

—MARIANNE
SAN FRANCISCO, CALIFORNIA

BEFORE I GAVE BIRTH, I thought it only happened to people who didn't want kids, had an unplanned pregnancy, were single parents or had a bad relationship with their partners. None of these applied to me. But within days of giving birth, I experienced such extreme PPD that I was beside myself. I was convinced that I'd made a horrible mistake in having the baby and wished someone else would take her! Fortunately, I had a very understanding gynecologist who diagnosed me and gave me some very fast-acting antidepressants. Within a week I was stabilized and after three months I began to bond and love my baby.

—ANONYMOUS
ALAMEDA, CALIFORNIA
7M

BEFORE THE BABY, I was very much into working long hours, making money, shopping, working out and making sure I looked good. Now that the baby is here, I still have over 20 pounds gained from the pregnancy after seven months, but I would prefer to stay with my daughter than to go to the gym and work out.

—MARIA FERRANTI
TORONTO, ONTARIO, CANADA
7M

. . . .

No matter what you do, your pre-baby life is never coming back.

—MARGARET KEENE
HERMOSA BEACH, CALIFORNIA
8M

. . . .

MY COLLEGE ROOMMATES AND I created a Mommy Group over the Internet. Between all of us, we've got nearly a dozen kids ranging from babies to teens. So no matter what question you have, somebody has some relevant experience they can share with you. Plus, it keeps us all in touch.

—K.B.
SAN FRANCISCO, CALIFORNIA
6 3 3M

FACT: RETAILERS STRATEGICALLY PLACE diapers near beer knowing full well that a man's quick run to the store for diapers can result in added purchases. Therefore, make sure you leave the man at home with the baby and you make the diaper run!

—MARTHA
SPRINGFIELD, ILLINOIS
😊17 👧12 😊7

• • • • • • • •

I THINK IT TAKES TIME AND PATIENCE for a woman to find her "mommy identity" and make peace with herself—with the body she is left with after a baby has been through it, with the lack of freedom, with the new responsibilities, with the change in your marriage relationship, and the changing roles as you become parents.

—SHER JOHNSON
EL SEGUNDO, CALIFORNIA
😊11 👧8 😊5.5M

• • • • • • • •

PEOPLE SAID, "IT'S GOING TO CHANGE YOUR LIFE," but no one prepared us for the massive emotional and social shift in our lives. You've got to change your whole way of being; suddenly you're focused on this one little individual and you're much less focused on each other.

—NANCY
PORTLAND, MAINE
👧2

REMEMBER S-E-X?

SEX AFTER BABY—WHAT A MILESTONE. The first time is an interesting experience, for sure. But it slowly gets back to what it was like before baby.

> —ADRIANE
> FT. LAUDERDALE, FLORIDA
>  1

• • • • • • • •

SEX WHILE BREASTFEEDING CAN BE SURPRISING. The first time we did it, we had warm, sticky milk all over us. It was quite a shock. We learned after that to let the kid eat, then make love.

> —V.B.
> DOHA, QATAR
> 👩 23 👩 21 👶 14

• • • • • • • •

WHEN THE DOCTORS SAY SIX WEEKS until you can start having sex again, they should really say two years. Then you'd feel good about the three times you did it last year!

> —SHAUNA
> VANCOUVER, BC, CANADA
> 👩 2 👩 8M

TONS OF PEOPLE WILL TELL YOU THAT IT'S IMPOSSIBLE, or difficult, to get pregnant while breastfeeding. Don't count on it. My mother got pregnant while still nursing a three-month old, and I got pregnant while nursing a seven-month old. Lucky for us, we both wanted those second babies, because the nursing certainly didn't prevent them from coming!

—SHANNON L.
SAN RAFAEL, CALIFORNIA
16 15 13

OUR SEX LIFE ISN'T VERY ACTIVE OR ROMANTIC at this point. We both work different hours at hospitals. And when we are alone, we have to do it quickly before the baby wakes up. Hopefully, it will get better once she sleeps through the night, but she's nine months old now, and is still getting up once or twice. I hope that by the time she does sleep through the night, my husband and I will still know how to be romantic.

—KELLY
JOLIET, ILLINOIS
1

BEFORE THE BABY, MY HUSBAND AND I used to walk to the local Dairy Queen some evenings for a sundae. One day after my baby was born, we were taking our walk and realized that we had forgotten all about our one-week old son: He was still at home by himself! That's when I realized that everything was different.

—PAGET PERRAULT
MELBOURNE, AUSTRALIA
👦35 👧30

. . . .

Never say, 'My child will never have a crusty nose,' or, 'I would never take my child out with a cough.'

—KELLI SCHARFF
SPRINGFIELD, ILLINOIS
👧19 👦17

. . . .

YOU MAY NOT BOND IMMEDIATELY with your new baby. Sometimes it takes a while to get used to being a mom. Don't feel you're inept or undeserving just because you're not instantly enamored with this little wrinkled, crying, pee-and-poop machine!

—ANONYMOUS
ALAMEDA, CALIFORNIA
👧7M

WE WERE STILL LIVING IN MY HUSBAND'S "bachelor pad" when the baby was born. It was hot, and, with our new addition, crowded. My husband called from work to say he was going to be 15 minutes late. When he walked in the door, I flipped out. I needed that time—even if it was only 15 minutes—for myself. My husband saw and smelled how everything was—the milk, the spit-up, the diapers, the heat—he said, "This used to be my Shangri-La." Having lost my 15 minutes of "alone time" and with hormones on the fritz, I responded, "This is my jail!"

—MARYBETH
SAN FRANCISCO, CALIFORNIA
4

• • • • • • • •

DON'T TAKE THE BABY SHOPPING or you will never buy anything for yourself again. Ask your husband to buy you a gift certificate to a boutique that sells women's clothing only and not cute little baby summer dresses.

—JANIE SCOTT
SAN ANTONIO, TEXAS
5M

INFANT INFO

There are more than twice as many 40-something moms now as there were 20 years ago.

BABY'S FAVORITE

I RECOMMEND THAT ALL DADS TAKE CARE of their kids, alone, for a large chunk of time: a whole day, a weekend—and not just once, but regularly. It gives them a chance to learn how to relate to the baby in their own unique way.

—JOHN KIM
LOS ANGELES, CALIFORNIA
 2

• • • • • • • •

FEED YOUR BABIES, CHANGE THEM, PLAY WITH THEM, take them for car rides, whatever puts the two of you together. When you walk in the house at the end of the day and hear "Dad-eeeeeeeee!" and a pair of little feet running to the door, it's an amazing feeling.

—LT. COL. DAVE EATON, USAF
FT. WALTON BEACH, FLORIDA
12 11

• • • • • • • •

ANYTHING PHYSICAL—TOSSING BABY IN THE AIR, swinging them, raspberries on tummy, severe tickling—will help you bond with your baby. Mom may not like it but baby sure will.

—MARK KAPLAN
FOSTER CITY, CALIFORNIA
3 1

LET YOUR BABY HEAR YOUR HEART. I used to lay our twins on my chest so they could listen to my heartbeat and fall asleep. I read somewhere that babies can get to know you this way.

—PAT BOEA
SYRACUSE, NEW YORK
19 17 15 12

DEVELOP A PRIVATE RITUAL WITH YOUR CHILD—something the two of you share that nobody else (including your spouse) does. When my daughter is done bathing, I wrap her up tightly in blankets and hold her close to me. It might sound simple, but moments such as these are crucial, because they're the foundation to build a lifetime of good memories upon.

—ANONYMOUS
CASTLE ROCK, COLORADO
3

DAD SHOULD BE LEFT ALONE WITH THE BABY, so he can't pass him or her off to his mom or someone else. Often, it is their insecurity about the baby that makes them hesitant to help with the baby care. Once they know they can do it, both you and he can relax.

—SHARI LEE SUGARMAN
NORTH BABYLON, NEW YORK
9w

DADS, BE GOOFY! Funny faces, funny voices, dancing, singing—I do it all.

> —DAN DUPONT
> ARLINGTON, VIRGINIA
> 👶6 👶3 👶3M

• • • • • • • •

WE HAVE A ROUTINE CALLED "FAMILY DANCING" that we started whenever my wife was away for the evening. Turn up your favorite music loud enough—but not too loud—that your child can hear the beat and "feel the sound." Hold your baby in your arms and gently dance, spin around, act silly, sing, and have fun. This continues to be a routine even though my baby is now 10 years old and has two little brothers.

> —TED RINEY
> DALLAS, TEXAS

HAVING KIDS CLOSE IN AGE is more difficult than having twins. At least twins are going through the same stages together and wearing the same size clothes and diapers! My girls are 15 months apart, and are always in slightly different stages.

—DONNA
ALLENTOWN, PENNSYLVANIA
7   6

• • • • • • • •

Don't underestimate how much energy it takes your wife to care for a newborn.

—ANONYMOUS
LIVERPOOL, NEW YORK
7   5

• • • • • • • • •

FATHERS GENERALLY TAKE TWO WEEKS of paternity leave after the birth. The problem is there isn't a tremendous amount a dad can do directly related to the baby. The mother is nursing nonstop and that's all the baby sees or wants. So my husband took his two weeks off and built a deck on the house. He felt it was the best, most productive use of his time, and it was the best expression of love possible.

—MARIANNE
SAN FRANCISCO, CALIFORNIA
4   5M

I'M THE ORGANIZER OF A DAD'S GROUP, and people are always asking me if I think there's a difference between dads and moms. In over six years of intensive interaction with full-time moms and full-time dads, I have determined that there is very little difference between the moms and dads, except that—on average—the dads drink significantly more beer.

—EVAN WEISSMAN
OAKLAND, CALIFORNIA
6 3

* * * * * * * *

BABIES SEEM TO REALIZE there's a difference between how Mommy and Daddy do things, and they accept both ways. My wife can make my baby giggle by kissing her all over, but she rarely laughs like that for me. I make her laugh by flying her through the air, but she almost never laughs when my wife does the same thing.

—JOHN KIM
LOS ANGELES, CALIFORNIA
2

* * * * * * * *

I ALWAYS GET UP AT NIGHT because I am breastfeeding, so my husband lets me sleep in one weekend morning. Just knowing I can sleep in makes me feel less tired. He also does a little more tidying up around the house in the evening so that we both get some time to relax.

—SHAUNA FARRELL
VANCOUVER, BC, CANADA
2 8M

After spending the day giving everything I have to the baby, I hate to say it, but there isn't a lot left for me to give to my husband.

—M.C.
FAIRFAX,
CALIFORNIA
11W

HUSBANDS, HELP YOUR WIVES with the night feedings. If your wife is breastfeeding, walk over to the nursery and bring the baby to her to nurse, and then carry the baby back to the nursery. Not only will this provide some much-needed relief for your wife, it will reinforce the feeling that you are a team.

—JAN
ALLENTOWN, PENNSYLVANIA
3 2

* * * * * * * *

TRY NOT TO GET JEALOUS IF YOUR MATE has better luck quieting down the baby, or if it seems like your newborn likes him more than you. Things have a way of shifting, and besides—you are in this together, for the long run, so try not to get petty.

—MOLLY F.
NEW YORK, NEW YORK

* * * * * * * *

I'VE FOUND THAT A LOT OF BABIES ARE COMFORTED by what my wife calls my "daddy magic." I just cradle the baby with my hand behind the child's head, my forearm beneath their back (so the baby's legs are on either side of my upper arm) and either rock them or pat/rub them gently with my left hand. There have been a number of social occasions where I've been called in from another room to rock an unhappy infant down for his/her nap.

—JAY JOHNSON
LANSING, MICHIGAN
13 11 8 20M

Whatever you do, never, EVER allow your husband to dress the baby.

—NICOLE LESSIN
HELOTES, TEXAS
17M

MY HUSBAND'S A VERY ORGANIZED GUY and, immediately after our daughter's birth, he didn't have any project to get accomplished. To stay busy he created an Excel spreadsheet of the baby's schedule—when she fed (and on which breast), when she pooped, when she slept. It was a great system. And when you speak to a pediatrician who asks when the last time your baby fed/pooped/slept, having readily available data is key.

—MARYBETH
SAN FRANCISCO, CALIFORNIA
4

> *I experience so much stress and worry all the time. I'm able to manage it by talking to my husband and remembering the good times.*
>
> —BETH
> OKLAHOMA
> 6

WHEN YOU COME HOME don't ask your wife, "What did you do today?" It sounds like you think she didn't do anything. Instead ask her, "How was your day?" And listen when she responds, even if it's all complaints.

—LEE MONTOPOLI
RIVER DALE, NEW JERSEY
3 5M

SINCE WE BECAME PARENTS, my husband has been amazing. He plans little overnight trips for us, leaves me love notes when he goes to work, and buys me flowers. When you have kids, one parent needs to take control of the relationship to make sure you make love and not break love.

—MARLA
BURBANK, CALIFORNIA
3 1

CONTROLLING THE VELVET ROPE

There will be many friends and relatives who feel they should have access to **your** baby. Although it is difficult, make some rules re: visitors and who can see and or hold **your** baby. As parents, you make the rules:

- No one with any possible contagious illness should be near your baby. That includes older siblings and other children who are most likely to have mild colds or other common childhood ailments.

- Washing hands (or using hand sanitizers) before touching your baby is a good idea.

- In the first few months, keep all contacts to a minimum. You know there are always certain folks who "need" to hold your baby. Be selective!

- Assure yourself that anyone who holds your baby knows how to do so gently, with good head support.

- All holders should use a towel or diaper on their shoulder so the baby will not come in contact with (or spit up on) their clothing.

If you are breast-feeding, your baby will have a more efficient immune system, but continue to limit contact with others to keep your baby from being exposed to common viral infections.

WHEN YOU HAVE AN OPPORTUNITY to be with your child, be there 100 percent. Forget the phone, forget the newspaper, forget the TV, forget washing the dishes, and forget eating if you can. You can do all those things after the baby goes to sleep.

—ARMIN BROTT
OAKLAND, CALIFORNIA
👶13 👶10 👶7M

• • • • • • • •

THE FIRST KID CHANGES YOUR WHOLE OUTLOOK on life. Being a father changes your responsibility to your family. I suddenly had a realization about my career, and I had to take a step back and consider where I was going, how to get serious and make real money.

—CHUCK S.
PONTE VEDRA BEACH, FLORIDA
👶9 👶4

INFANT INFO

If you thought it was coincidence that a baby begins to stir when mommy walks into the room, think again. Newborns can recognize the smell of their mothers' breast milk.

ONE NIGHT MY FRIEND STEVE was over. I was holding my son, and he threw up all over me. My wife yelled, "Quick, get a rag!" So Steve ran to the kitchen, got a rag, and started cleaning me off. Then my wife yelled, "No, not him—the rug!" That gave me a pretty good sense of my status.

—JOEL ROSENFELD
NEW YORK, NEW YORK
👤 😷 17 😷 16

• • • • • • • • •

Every Wednesday night is Papa night. They do something special without Mommy—mostly things that Mommy doesn't like to do.

—ANONYMOUS
LAGUNA BEACH, CALIFORNIA
😊 2

• • • • • • • • •

WHEN MY BABY WAS BORN, my husband became very involved. He worked most of the day, but at night when the baby cried, he picked him up, put him in the sling, and walked with him for hours.

—GINA
HOUSTON, TEXAS
😊 2

THE BEST ADVICE I GOT when I had my baby was from my father. He said that I should always remember that I am a wife first and a mom second, and not to forget to make my husband a priority. I never forgot this and I do it today. My husband and I are the mold and the kids just follow our shape and form. So if we love and respect each other, then everything else just falls into place.

—ANONYMOUS
LAS VEGAS, NEVADA
😊6 👶1

> There's nothing like a long day at the office to make a man realize how much he misses his baby.
>
> —ARMIN BROTT
> OAKLAND,
> CALIFORNIA
> 👶 13
> 👶 10
> 👶 7M

I AM A STAY-AT-HOME MOM, but my husband takes half of the responsibility for our kids when he gets home from work. He does most of the nighttime reading and bathing. I feel sorry for women whose husbands think that because they bring home a paycheck, they deserve to have free time at the end of the day. Taking care of children is a job, too.

—ANONYMOUS
FT. LAUDERDALE, FLORIDA
😊5 👶2

MY HUSBAND IS A PRO AT BURPING and a pro at changing the dirtiest of the diapers, which I always give to him. He never gets flustered when the baby cries and keeps a level head at all times.

—REINA
HOLLYWOOD, CALIFORNIA
😊1

MY HUSBAND HAS BEEN GREAT in the dad role. He saw my daughter and me through a difficult entry into this world and has been our constant support ever since. When we first got home, my husband insisted on sweeping the entire house every night (we have hardwood floors). I giggled to myself and thought it might be short-lived (I was right; it lasted about a week after we got home) but I really appreciated his concern and the clean house. Our daughter is already two months old, and he's still the man in charge of cleaning!

—ELIZABETH
GAINESVILLE, FLORIDA
2M

Your pediatrician may recommend the parenting books written by the American Academy of Pediatrics. Considered to be some of the best general parenting advice texts available, they are *Caring for Your Baby and Young Child: Birth to Age 5 (Fourth Edition)* and *Your Baby's First Year (Second Edition)*. Written by pediatricians, these books offer practical, easy-to-follow advice for new parents. The information has been evaluated and refined by the most important organization of pediatricians in the world. The AAP website also has excellent health and parenting advice: http://www.AAP.org.

MY HUSBAND UNDERSTANDS THAT MY FOCUS is entirely on our children, so he works really hard to make sure that we get alone time together, even if it's only an hour. He gets his parents to come over and takes me on a picnic or out to dinner. Sometimes he'll just rent a private room for us somewhere, even though we can't spend the night. He's worked so hard and continues to work to make sure that our relationship and sex life doesn't falter.

—JILLIAN
TEMPE, ARIZONA
1

. . . .

MY HUSBAND USED TO WORK PAST SEVEN AT NIGHT, but since our daughter was born, he's been home at five-thirty on the dot every night. And when he gets home, he immediately relieves me and takes her for a long walk. And he does it with a smile on his face.

—ANONYMOUS
SANTA MONICA, CALIFORNIA
2

. . . .

ONE OF THE BIGGEST MISTAKES I made was expecting Dad to pick up 50 percent of the slack. As a mom, you are the primary caregiver; you have to accept that and get used to it. There is no equality and I don't think there really can be, especially if you are nursing.

—MICHAEL BETTI
VENICE, CALIFORNIA
1

MY HUSBAND WAS GREAT when my son was born, and he gets better and better. When I got home from the hospital, he took three weeks off from work and took over everything except breast-feeding. For three weeks, the only responsibility I had was feeding. He changed diapers, prepared meals for us, and cleaned. He works full time, so he can't be my around-the-clock nurse and caretaker, but when he is around he is completely focused on what he can do for me and for our son.

—DANI
HOLLYWOOD, FLORIDA
2

• • • • • • • •

MY HUSBAND DIDN'T REALIZE how much work it was to raise a baby, until I decided to go back to work and left him home as a stay-at-home dad. The first day I came home to a screaming baby, a tired husband and a house that looked like a tornado went through it. After about a week things started getting better and now he even offers to stay with the baby when I get home from work. I think men just have to be forced to take care of the kids without any help from us. When we try to get involved, they feel like we are treating them like children.

—ANONYMOUS
LAS VEGAS, NEVADA
6 1

One of the most surprising things to me as a new parent was the sheer amount of love I had for my new daughter. I never knew I could love anything so much.

*—WAYNE DRASH
ATLANTA,
GEORGIA*
2

I HAD THE NEW-MOTHER BLUES after I had my son. One night, he wouldn't fall asleep. I fed him, changed his diaper, and I played with him, but he would not stop yelling at the top of his lungs. Then I called my mom, telling her the situation in my teary-eyed voice. She told me to bring the baby over so I could get some rest. She watched my son for the next couple days. After that, he never made me cry again. I always wondered what she did to him.

—BARBARA ROBINSON
CHICAGO, ILLINOIS
👶10 👶5

• • • • • • • •

MY HUSBAND DIDN'T STEP into his father role immediately, but now he has it down and it's great. It was a real struggle at first—until I stopped telling him how to do things. I had to learn that my way isn't always the right way and I had to let him figure things out on his own. Men don't like to be told what to do, so ladies, watch what you get when you take a hands-off approach with them.

—J.F.
SEATTLE, WASHINGTON
👶3

My husband helps me by letting me have time to myself and taking care of the girls when I need a break.

—CASSIE
DEMILLE
FAIRCHILD
AFB,
WASHINGTON
👶2 👶2M

MY HUSBAND IS IN THE NAVY. Before he went overseas for six months, he worried that our son wouldn't remember him. He thought that if my son could smell his dad on some things in the house—a blanket, a T-shirt—that would help him remember. Then, while my husband was overseas, he sent video cards at least twice a month. My husband is back now and I really believe that my son recognized him; as soon as we picked up my husband, my son smiled and clapped his hands!

—ANONYMOUS
MAMMOTH LAKES, CALIFORNIA
1

MY HUSBAND CAME UP WITH A DADDY CHECKLIST, and sent it to all of his friends. He says the most important things to remember as a new dad are: pick your battles carefully; choose your child over cleaning; hold and hug your baby every chance you get; tell them you love them all of the time; tell them they are special, beautiful and smart. These are my husband's mottoes, and he lives by every single one of them.

—ANONYMOUS
MINNEAPOLIS, MINNESOTA
1

MY HUSBAND COULDN'T WAIT TO BE A FATHER. He was so frustrated by the fact that there were all of these women's support groups but nothing for men, so he started his own group. Once a month he meets with other fathers in our neighborhood to talk about the trials and joys of fatherhood.

—ANONYMOUS
PACIFIC PALISADES, CALIFORNIA
3

· · · · · · · ·

MY HUSBAND IS A GREAT FATHER, but it took me a while to see it. When we had our first child, we both worked, so at the end of our days we had to both take on an equal amount of child care responsibilities. I always felt like I was doing more, and he, like he was doing more. We started keeping score, and it got really ugly. It became this battle of egos. One day, I realized that we were both working really hard to make things work and I tossed out my scorecard.

—ANONYMOUS
HOUSTON, TEXAS
1 7 3

The Real World: Work, Family & Life

In most families, the enormous adjustment of settling in with a newborn is quickly followed by the enormous adjustment of returning to a regular work and home schedule that now includes a baby.

Ideally, one parent is able to stay at home with the newborn baby for as long as possible, but state and workplace laws concerning parental leave vary greatly. Whatever the length of leave available to you, take all of it. In addition, many new parents find they can work from home, have flexible hours, or work a different schedule. Some parents are willing and able to make a shift in their work situation that continues through the first year.

But for some parents, it's just too difficult, practically and, sometimes, emotionally, to turn over the care of an infant to anyone else. These parents will need to find another option, which may be a leave of absence from work, a transfer to part-time work, or a decision to re-enter the workforce when the child is older. Remember, there's no one right answer to the work/family dilemma; each family finds its own best solution.

WORK TOGETHER. Raising a child, especially during those first years, should be a team effort. Gone are the days when the mother took on all the responsibilities of child rearing. It's hard work, with many challenges and unbelievable rewards, all of which should be shared by both parents.

—LAURA KRONEN
NEW YORK, NEW YORK
👶15M

Get a sales job so that you can work from home!

—J.H.
MILL VALLEY,
CALIFORNIA
👶 9

. . . .

IT IS ABSOLUTELY POSSIBLE TO HAVE A CAREER and raise a family. But a woman has to make the decision that she is going to work hard to be a mother to her baby and pursue her career. Every day I asked myself if I had been a good mother to my baby and done a good job at work. Yes, this is difficult, but it can be done.

—PAT Q.T.
OAKLAND, CALIFORNIA
👶32 👶27

. . . .

GO TO ANY LENGTHS NECESSARY to have someone you know watch your children. When we needed a person to care for our children, we went to the wife of the deacon who married us even though she lives some distance away. For us, the security and welfare of our kids was the number one priority.

—RICK BARBERO
GAITHERSBURG, MARYLAND
👶12 👶5

WHEN SELECTING A DAY CARE PROVIDER, drop in unexpectedly to see what the place is really like. Look for a facility that is clean and where the children are happy. Watch how the caregivers interact with the children. Ask lots of questions. Don't worry about asking something that will offend them—the treatment of your child is more important. Find out the beliefs of the caregivers, how they discipline, their teaching styles and how they feel about issues that are important to you. If you have any doubts, it probably isn't the place to take your most precious treasure.

—STACEY HATFIELD
ANAHUAC, TEXAS
4

Babies make you add weird 'eeee' sounds to the end of your words. 'The doggie went to sleepy.' Be careful when in professional settings to remove the 'eeee' from your words.

—TILLY
CHAMPAIGN, ILLINOIS
15

WHEN I GET HOME, I PRETTY MUCH GIVE ALL my attention to the kids because I don't get to see them all day. The other stuff you think is important—work around the house— can wait. It's not as important when you put it in perspective with how fleeting those moments with your kids are.

—KEN BECKERING
SYRACUSE, NEW YORK
👶5 👶2

• • • • • • • •

AFTER HAVING OUR SECOND CHILD I went back to work full-time, so we hired a nanny who's at our home 50 hours a week. Mothering my children is the highest priority, so yes, I wish I spent more time at home. And yet, I also find work stimulating, challenging and rewarding.

—A.D.
SAN FRANCISCO, CALIFORNIA
👶3 👶1

• • • • • • • •

I STAYED HOME WHEN MY DAUGHTER was growing up. I thought that it was important for me or my husband to be home, but we made some tough choices to do that. It took us longer to save for a house, for instance. We lived in a one-bedroom, third-floor apartment until our daughter went to kindergarten.

—BETTY
LOWER SAUCONY, PENNSYLVANIA
👶34

YOU MIGHT BE SURPRISED TO DISCOVER that it is possible to stay home with your kids, if that's what you want to do. I am a scientist, so I had a hard time imagining how I could possibly work from home. But I do! I work from home as a consultant for pharmaceutical companies and health insurance companies, do medical writing, and lecture at a university. If you can be creative, there are lots of opportunities out there to work from home. You can start your own business, do Tupperware, the sky's the limit. I figure if I can do it, anyone can!

—KELLY KARPA
PENNSYLVANIA
👦5 👧3

• • • • • • • •

Get dads involved early. They aren't trying to escape from helping; they are just overwhelmed and don't know where to begin.

—ERICA CAMARA
WHITEMAN AIR FORCE BASE, MISSOURI
🐾17M

THE FIRST TIME I LEFT MY BABY SON with a sitter, I became aware that Mother Nature controls more than I suspected. The entire time I was away from my baby, my mind and body were aware every second that a) my son was somewhere else, and b) I didn't know if he was perfectly OK. Even though the sitter was a trusted employee of my husband's, I could not shake the constant feeling that I should be back home with him. Consequently, my forays from home were brief initially.

—JANNY TANG
SANTA CRUZ, CALIFORNIA
31

· · · · · · · · · ·

I FOUND OUR BABYSITTER THROUGH SOMEONE who used to clean my house. I trusted my former housekeeper's opinion, but I still did my research. I met my babysitter several times before we hired her, and I watched her interact with my children. She was good natured and made direct eye contact. Plus I knew she had raised four children of her own.

—LISA ANGELETTIE, M.S.W.
ENGLEWOOD, NEW JERSEY
5 3 2

It's very hard to go from working full-time to staying home all day. A spouse needs to be supportive and help out with diapers and baths and other household chores. Mine doesn't.

—M.
EDGEWATER,
MARYLAND
4 3M

IT TAKES TWO

AT FIRST, MY WIFE GOT IRRITATED WITH ME when I would
have her take the kids every time I needed to get something done. She pointed out that she didn't have that
luxury during the week when I was at work, and I should
learn to deal with kids and life simultaneously. So, I've
had to become more proficient at multitasking—a kid on
the lap while at the computer, feeding the kids while
talking on the phone.

—J.R.
CHICAGO, ILLINOIS
😊4 😊2 😊1

• • • • • • • •

WHEN IT WAS JUST OUR FIRST CHILD, I did more of my
share of housekeeping than I had normally
done. (Of course, this would mean I had
done something to begin with, so anything at that point was an improve-
ment.) But housework was only half of
what I needed to do to be helpful. You
also have to make sure you're there emotionally, with as much understanding as
you can give.

—DAVID E. LISS
PENNINGTON, NEW JERSEY
😊4 😊1

SINCE I DID CHILD CARE WHILE WORKING FROM HOME on weekdays, my husband had full child care responsibility (except for nursing, of course!) when he came home from work at night, and on weekends. Plus, he made dinner when he got home from work. When he told a female acquaintance about our arrangement, she said, "But you've been working all day! You need to rest!" His reply: "So has she—at two jobs!" Wonderful man!

—KATHARINE O'MOORE-KLOPF
EAST SETAUKET, NEW YORK
21 9 2

WHEN OUR CHILDREN WERE BORN, I HAD A JOB that required inordinately long hours. But, when I finally did get home, I made it a point to plunge in. Sure, I was tired. But what about my wife, who had coped all day? I'd help with the baths, feedings, diaper changing, story time. I'd take care of them on my days off so my wife could get out by herself. It made a huge difference in my wife being able to survive the rigors of motherhood.

—DOUGLAS S. LOONEY
BOULDER, COLORADO
37 34

I TOOK A ONE-YEAR SABBATICAL WHEN MY DAUGHTER was about three and my son was a year. I was working on my own projects, but I took total responsibility for picking them up, dropping them off, taking them to the doctor. It was tremendous. The best part of it was developing a relationship with my kids.

—ANONYMOUS
BETHESDA, MARYLAND
👩 9 👦 6

• • • • • • • •

WHEN I GOT HOME FROM WORK, THE FIRST THING I DID was pick up my boy to give my wife a break. When I did this on a regular basis, she stopped nagging me about petty little things. It's a very worthwhile exchange.

—ROBERT HARRIS
LOS ANGELES, CALIFORNIA
👩 26 👦 17

WHEN BOTH PARENTS WORK, it must be a shared responsibility. At first, I'd stay at work a little late—just 30 minutes longer than usual. I'd come home and see my wife's stress. She had picked up the kids and gone home. Our daughter needed her diaper changed. Dinner needed to be started. And our son was crying for attention. We decided that we needed to come home at the same time. Then, each of us could handle some of the responsibilities.

—CHRIS GRAHAM
SYRACUSE, NEW YORK
😊4 👶1

* * * * * * * * *

IF YOU WANT TO WORK FROM HOME, plan on getting some extra child care, even if it's only a teenage helper to keep an eye on your baby while you work in another room. I had planned on working from home after my baby was born, squeezing it in during my daughter's naps. But I discovered that naptimes are about the only time you can get anything done: housework, cooking, sleeping, relaxing, reading. Forcing myself to hop on the computer during those precious few hours when I wanted to do everything else was difficult.

—MELODY WARNICK
ST. GEORGE, UTAH
👶2

Go through an accredited babysitting agency. But still go with your gut instincts. If you think something is not quite right about a sitter, you're probably right.

—LISA ARMONY
SHERMAN OAKS,
CALIFORNIA
😊5 😊2 🐕

WHEN YOU'RE CHOOSING A BABYSITTER, have him/her over to your house for an hour or so while you're there. Stay close enough that you can hear and/or see what's going on, but far enough away that your child and the babysitter don't include you in their interaction. You'll have a pretty good sense of whether it's the right fit or not.

—DEBORAH FISHER
FORT WASHINGTON, PENNSYLVANIA
9M

We set up a system to reduce stress: Every night, one parent was allowed one hour to go shopping, take a bath, get some exercise, whatever. The next night was the other person's turn.

—MICHAEL
ST. PAUL, MINNESOTA
11 5

MY HUSBAND WAS EXCELLENT ABOUT HELPING me out. In fact, he seemed to make a better mother than I did when it came to handling the feedings/changings so expertly!

—BEV PORTER
COLORADO SPRINGS, COLORADO
14 11

AFTER MY FIRST NANNY WANTED TO BE PAID two full weeks while our family was on vacation without her, I decided to make a "nanny handbook." It spelled out everything—from what the baby could eat to how much TV the other kids could watch. There was even a section in it that entitled me to three "free days" where I could cancel the nanny if my mother or mother-in-law wanted to take the kids for a day. Nannies had to agree to the conditions and sign a "contract." I also made the nannies keep a logbook of the activities around the house so I could see what my kids were doing. That way, I knew what to expect when I was home.

—SUZANNE DAUGHERTY
ARLINGTON HEIGHTS, ILLINOIS
7 5 2

* * * * * * * *

AFTER THEY'VE JUST EATEN, WATCH OUT! I came home from work one day at lunchtime wearing a pure white uniform. I picked up my two-week old son and started playing with him. All of a sudden, I felt this warmth all over my chest. He had completely soiled my shirt, and I barely had enough time to change clothes before getting back to the office.

—MARK SCOTT
SAFFORD, ARIZONA
16 13

FOR THE FIRST WEEK AFTER MY WIFE RETURNED to work we went together to take our daughter to and from day care. We did that more for us than for her, so that we would both know the routine. I felt very sad to leave her because I didn't know how she would react to the new situation. It turns out she was very happy to be there, but I was sad.

> —DANIEL H. AMINOFF
> ALEXANDRIA, VIRGINIA
> 5M

· · · · · · · · ·

TWO WEEKS AFTER MY C-SECTION my company told me they needed me to come to Hawaii to do an advertisement. They told me to bring my baby and husband, so I said, "Absolutely! I'm there, no problem." I was probably still doped up at the time and thinking that I was healed. Twenty-four hours later I was in the most excruciating pain and somehow, later that week, I was supposed to be hiking down cliffs to oversee a photo shoot. There was just no way.

> —MARGARET KEENE
> HERMOSA BEACH, CALIFORNIA
> 8M

Spend a lot of time with your children, even if you're a working mother. Quality time with your child is extremely important. These are the most influential years of their life.

—*MICHELLE HIRSCH ATLANTA, GEORGIA 8*

TRYING TO BALANCE WORK WITH FAMILY, I just got used to being exhausted. I still have visions of myself driving to work in the morning at about seven a.m., having just dropped off two kids at two different places and feeling so tired it was hard to believe I was just starting the day. But I did fine at work once I was there, and I managed to handle everything, so I think we just adapt.

— BARBARA STEWART
SEATTLE, WASHINGTON
⊛20 ⚤17

• • • • • • • • •

IF PEOPLE CAN AFFORD IT, I REALLY RECOMMEND one parent work only part-time. When my youngest son was born, I went back to work full-time right away. It was so hard, sometimes I wonder how I got through it. A few months later, I had the opportunity to change jobs and work only part time. When I asked my husband about it, he said, "Do you even need to ask?" There was no question; it was the best thing for our family.

— TRUDY
PERKASIE, PENNSYLVANIA
⚤59 ⊛57 ⊛46 ⊛40

PICTURE, VIDEO, AND THE INTERNET

TAKE A PICTURE OF THE BABY EACH MONTH on the date of his birth for the whole first year. I also try to tape a 10-minute video of my son once a week, nothing special; I just film him throughout the day doing whatever he's doing.

—ROBYN
BIGLERVILLE, PENNSYLVANIA
👶1

· · · · · · · · ·

INSTEAD OF TRYING TO WAIT FOR ONE GREAT VIDEO moment, take lots of little videos of everyday things. After a year, you'll have all sorts of great footage that you can edit together—the baby rolling over or eating, or even just sitting and crying. It will be a great thing to look back at when your child is older.

—ELLIS
SEATTLE, WASHINGTON
👵1

· · · · · · · · ·

FOR A GOOD PICTURE, GET CLOSE. For a better picture, get closer.

—M. ALLEN
ATLANTA, GEORGIA
👵6 👶3

WHEN YOU DECIDE IT'S TIME TO TAKE BABY to the photographer's studio to get his or her picture taken, do it after the baby has eaten and napped. Otherwise they can be all fussy and fidgety. They tend to be much more cooperative if their belly is full and they're not tired.

—ANONYMOUS
BRUNSWICK, OHIO
👶5 👶4

A PROFESSIONAL PHOTOGRAPHER ONCE TOLD ME that when you take still portraits of your kids, keep their eyes in the upper third of the picture because it balances the photo and makes the kid the center of attention.

—STEPHANIE ISMERT
CENTENNIAL, COLORADO
👶8 👶6 👶1

AT LEAST TWO PEOPLE ARE REQUIRED to take a good baby picture—one to hold the baby and one to make funny faces and to push the button. I have found that raising the baby up in the air makes him smile, so my wife gets in position underneath and we get good Superbaby shots.

—DAN DUPONT
ARLINGTON, VIRGINIA
👶6 👶3 👶3M

WHEN I WENT BACK TO WORK after four months, things became intensely stressful. I was doing most of the work at home in addition to working a full day. My husband and I snapped at one another and started taking each other for granted. After a huge falling out—which we never had before—he realized that he had to pitch in more. Now he helps out so much and a lot of the burden has been lifted from me. It's all about finding the balance of time for myself, time for our daughter, and time for my husband. I also needed to learn to ask for help and not be Supermom, and not feel guilty. It was a huge maturation process for me.

—A.S.
11M

• • • • • • • • •

I TOOK MY WIFE TO PARIS as a surprise Valentine's Day present after our daughter was born. We left the baby with my mom. We called from the road on the way to the airport, from the airport, from the plane, when we arrived, from the hotel. I am proud to report we didn't call to check on her from the Eiffel Tower. But we probably talked about whether we should.

—ALLAN JAFFE
PETALUMA, CALIFORNIA
21 6

ALL NEW MOTHERS SHOULD FORCE THEMSELVES to be apart from their babies sometime within the first six months. I didn't trust anyone to take care of my firstborn and I refused to leave him with anybody. Then, my son had to get his tonsils taken out, and moms weren't allowed to stay at the hospital, so we were separated for two whole nights. It was so traumatic that I went home and cried my eyes out.

> —JANIS HACKETT
> CENTENNIAL, COLORADO
> 👶36 👶32 👶26 👶24

• • • • • • • • •

PLACES TO FIND GOOD SITTERS ARE CHURCHES and universities. The university in our town has a list of students in child and human development classes who want to babysit because they need the experience for their majors. Two college girls that we found this way ended up having roommates who also became good babysitters for our kids.

> —JILL
> FORT COLLINS, COLORADO
> 👶7 👧3

• • • • • • • • •

I USED SEVERAL OF THE BABY EINSTEIN DVDs. I don't really know if they made her any smarter, but I was able to get dinner started.

> —JULI KEDROWSKI
> MAINEVILLE, OHIO
> 👶 4 👧 6

WHEN IT COMES TO BABYSITTING, I am appalled at how little most people are willing to pay for it. You are leaving your precious child's very life in the hands of someone else; is this not worth more than the price of a couple of movie tickets? We overpaid greatly on purpose because we wanted her sitters to know how much we valued their time and skills.

—KATHLEEN JUN MAGYAR
DALLAS, TEXAS
18

It's amazing how many things you can get done with one hand. You really master that while you're holding a baby in one arm!

—MICHELE CONTIS
FAIRFAX,
CALIFORNIA
11w

HERE'S MY ABSOLUTE NUMBER ONE piece of advice for stay-at-home parents: Get together with other stay-at-home parents! The isolation of being alone with a baby can drive you crazy. Finding those parents and sharing the joys, stresses, excitement, and challenges of parenting is the best thing you can do for yourself.

—EVAN WEISSMAN
OAKLAND, CALIFORNIA
6 3

I MADE A MISTAKE WHEN MY KIDS were younger by not spending enough time with them. If you work all day long, cut down to half a day or you'll miss out on a lot. It's beautiful to be with a child.

—B.
LOS ANGELES, CALIFORNIA

IF NOT YOU, WHO?

Inevitably, you will need child care. Either you are returning to work, or you need to go somewhere without your child for a period of time. Even if you don't need it now, it's never too soon to research and plan your child care options.

If you must go back to work, some companies have on-site day care. Check the age restrictions, safety record, size, and costs, if any, and compare them to other day care choices in your neighborhood; you may decide you prefer a different day care arrangement than the one the company offers.

Talk to other parents in your area about their day care arrangements and any other options they may know about. Interview all prospective caregivers, get references, and *follow up on them*. Make sure the caregivers have the same philosophy of child care as you do. Plan on making unexpected visits to evaluate your caregiver's skills. Don't hesitate to change caregivers if you are not comfortable. Finding the right situation can be difficult and time-consuming, but worth the effort.

I STAYED AT HOME WITH MY KIDS until they were five years old, independent and off to kindergarten. Then I went back to work. Parenting is a unique experience; you can always work, so I really cherished those years that they were infants.

—GLORIA RIVERA
BURLINGAME, CALIFORNIA
21 20 16 10 1M

. . . .

I felt guilty about not spending more time with my baby. Then I realized that the quantity of time spent with my child was not as important as the quality of our experiences.

—SUZANNE
FORT COLLINS, COLORADO
4

. . . .

MAKE SURE THE BABYSITTER has good references and does a lot with the kids, not just stick them in front of the TV. The one I have now takes them outside every day (weather permitting), does art projects, reads books, and teaches them things.

—LAUREN HIDDEN
NEW CUMBERLAND, PENNSYLVANIA
4 2

I RUN THE HOUSEHOLD, AS FAR AS LAUNDRY, cooking, cleaning, etc. My husband, however, is very involved with playtime, bath time, diapering, feeding and all aspects of child care. On the weekends, we share all responsibilities and he is a very hands-on daddy. He'll also spend alone time with each of the children. I think this makes for everyone being happier.

—VANESSA WILKINSON
COLORA, MARYLAND
👶3 👶5M

• • • • • • • •

I MADE SURE THAT LEAVING MY DAUGHTER at day care the first time wasn't horrible by making sure I didn't do it when I was returning to work. I did a couple practice runs where I just left her for three hours or so. I was working from home during that time, so I also had things to keep me busy and not focused on worrying about her.

—JULIE KIND
ARLINGTON, VIRGINIA
👶6M

• • • • • • • •

DON'T BE AFRAID TO REACH OUT FOR HELP. We hired a "doula," which is the German term for someone who helps with the baby, cooking and cleaning. She's a nanny, a housekeeper and can do anything we need, from preparing a meal to changing the baby.

—G.P.
MINNEAPOLIS, MINNESOTA
👶2M

My husband and I laugh about how two intelligent people can carry on a conversation over dinner about poopy and super soaker diapers.

— MICHELLE LEWIS
PLANTATION,
FLORIDA
👶2M

ONE PARENT SHOULD WORK FROM HOME. My husband is a writer, so he was often at home and available to help with our daughter. I don't know how I would have handled life if he wasn't available to help during the day. While a babysitter or nanny may still be necessary, the work-at-home parent can be a secure presence to the child.

—E.G.
NEW HAVEN, CONNECTICUT
20

• • • • • • • •

SET THE WORKLOAD BALANCE UP FRONT. Don't expect your husband to be considerate; don't expect him to be the one to get up in the middle of the night. I told him I needed time for myself on weekends. That caused a lot of fights. He would say, "I work full-time." I would respond with, "What do you think I'm doing?"

—ISABELLA
SANTA CRUZ, CALIFORNIA
18M

• • • • • • • •

AFTER EACH KID IS BORN, IT'S ALWAYS HARD when I go back to my job. My husband works days and I work nights as a pharmacist, so we've been able to share duties and avoid most paid child care. But it's still difficult not being home. I get calls like, "Don't worry, honey, but where is the medical insurance card?" So many of the calls start with, "Don't worry, honey, but . . ."

—PILAR SHOAP
ABINGDON, MARYLAND
7 4 2 3M

I HAD MY CHILDREN WITH ME ALL DAY LONG. My husband would come home, and I'd want him to take the baby because I needed a break. They'd start crying and instead of trying to deal with it and play with them or walk with them or rock them or get on the floor with them, he'd say, "They don't like me." Then he'd hand them back. He'd change poopy diapers with no complaint. But aside from that, it was hard for him.

—ANDREA
GRAND LAKE, COLORADO
🐶9 🐾5

* * * * * * * *

HIRE SOMEONE TO HELP CLEAN THE HOUSE. When the baby's sleeping, the last thing you want to do is clean, but that's what you end up doing. I felt like I was always cleaning and nothing was ever really clean, and I didn't have any time for myself. It's really not that expensive, maybe the cost of a dinner out once a month. If you can swing it, it's so worth it!

—MARY WALSH
CINCINNATI, OHIO
🐾 6 🐾 4 🐾 1 🐶 7

* * * * * * * *

WHEN PEOPLE SAY THEY WANT TO SEE YOUR BABY pictures, they want to see one picture. They do not want to look through 10 albums with a thousand pictures each.

—DEB
ORONO, MAINE
🐶18

BE FLEXIBLE. I try to plan out my days, but with a baby sometimes it just doesn't work. Each night I make a list of the things I hope to do the next day. It makes me feel really good when I check things off of it. But it doesn't always work out that way, so I've learned to be flexible.

—JILL
SHOEMAKERSVILLE, PENNSYLVANIA
👶11M

• • • • • • • •

WITH THREE KIDS ALL UNDER the age of five, there was no such thing as sharing the load—the load was all mine! My husband had just started his own business and was gone day and night, 24/7. Some days my nerves would be totally shot by 10:00 in the morning. When I did get time to myself I would indulge in an alcoholic beverage (usually a beer), and write in my journal. This was one of the things that saved my sanity. I also had a friend that was a stay-at-home mom. We would call each other up while making our dinner and having our drinks together over the phone. It was nice to know someone else was experiencing the same frustration, loneliness and isolation.

—S.C.
BRAMPTON, ONTARIO, CANADA
👦17 👦15 👶12

AS MY HUSBAND WAS THE ONE GOING OUT to work each day and I was a stay-at-home mom, I did most of the workload. Organization is the key to it all, as is planning ahead. I keep a calendar on my computer and on my fridge to help keep me on top of things.

—LYNDA DIFRANCESCO
RALEIGH, NORTH CAROLINA
2 2M

* * * * * * * *

I FOUND THAT IT WAS ACTUALLY EASIER to work from home in the first month than it was in the following months. While the baby was sleeping I could do a lot. In later months, when the baby needed more interaction, it was harder to get anything done.

—BRETTE SEMBER
CLARENCE, NEW YORK
12 6

* * * * * * * *

ONCE I WENT BACK TO WORK, we had to take turns doing everything. I would do a load of laundry in the morning and he would put one in at night. If I cooked, he cleaned the kitchen. If I swept the floors, he vacuumed. While I nursed, he would get her bath stuff ready. We had to learn how to work as a team.

—STACEY HATFIELD
ANAHUAC, TEXAS
4

LIVE CLOSE TO YOUR PARENTS OR SOMEONE that can babysit for free. It will save you so much money in the long run, and probably save your relationship as well, because you will feel like you can go out together, alone, more often.

—TOCCA
BROOKLYN, NEW YORK

• • • • • • • •

IF YOU'RE THE STAY-AT-HOME PARENT, you will be doing a lot more. There's no way around it. I work from home so I feel like I get stuck with most of the housework, because I can do bits here and there throughout the day. I feel like I'm never really "off," but it's hard to ask him to do more when he comes home from work and he's tired, too.

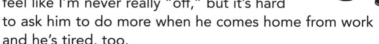

—SHAUNA FARRELL
VANCOUVER, BC, CANADA
2 8M

Get a nanny.

*—SHARON
MUALEM
ATLANTA,
GEORGIA*
4 1

• • • • • • • •

I WENT TO MY HAIRDRESSER THE OTHER DAY with my hair pulled back in a banana clip and she said, "You look like such a mom!" Inside, I thought, "Oh, God, no! Not a mom!" I guess the moral of the story is that if you want to stay cool, don't wear banana clips. Or overalls.

—STEPHANIE ISMERT
CENTENNIAL, COLORADO
8 6 1

GET A BABYSITTER ASAP—within six months. My spouse and I go out one night a week together and we each get "a night off."

> —TRACEY G.
> SAN FRANCISCO, CALIFORNIA
> 3

· · · · · · · ·

MY DAUGHTER WAS ABOUT TWO MONTHS OLD and I took her to the store with me. I got out of the car to take her out of her car seat and realized the doors had locked with the keys inside. I immediately called my husband for help; then I sat on the hood of my car and cried and thought about what a horrible mother I was. About five minutes into my cry, I realized that my car keys were in my pocket.

> —ANONYMOUS
> FT. LEE, NEW JERSEY
> 2

· · · · · · · · ·

FOR GOD'S SAKE, THEY'RE CUTE—just watch them. I think there is this feeling that everything has to be document-ed—you know, the first haircut, the first everything. And that documentation becomes more important than the event itself. I think a lot of people miss a lot of things because they're so busy taking pictures they don't actually see what's going on.

> —DEB
> ORONO, MAINE
> 18

DON'T STOP DOING THE THINGS YOU LOVE TO DO. I still
shop, go to restaurants, dance and travel, yet I am a mom.

—L.G.
WEST NEW YORK, NEW JERSEY
2

. . . .

LIKE EVERYTHING ELSE, WE TRIED TO SPLIT the workload
evenly. Since my wife is a light sleeper, and it takes a lot to
wake me up, she responded to his late night cries most of
the time. However, on those occasions where she was too
exhausted or simply didn't feel like getting up, a sharp
elbow to my sides was usually enough to get me out of bed.

—JOHN RODGERS
SEATTLE, WASHINGTON
9

. . . .

I E-MAIL MY PARENTS ROUTINELY about milestones and
funny things that happen. My mother, in particular, loves
them. She's far away and, like me, on the computer all
day, so e-mails about her grandkids are absolute
treasures. What's more, these little e-mails
and the responses they elicit make great
baby book fodder. I'm notoriously bad at
keeping up with such books, so I hoard
e-mails and print out the ones about
the kids for inclusion.

—DAN DUPONT
ARLINGTON, VIRGINIA
6 3 3M

*Don't get
rid of your
hip clothes
once you
stop fitting
into them.
They will
serve as
reminders
of your
days of hip-
ness.*

—ANONYMOUS
STOCKDALE,
TEXAS
2 7M

WHEN MY DAUGHTER WAS BORN I LAUNCHED a "family news" Web site. I made it funny! And silly! And cute! But not too silly or cute. And I gave it video and picture galleries. In short, it was a place where my family and friends could log on, and witness the growth of our daughter, and later, our son. I wrote mercifully short news articles on developments in their lives, and funny articles on how parenthood had changed me and my wife. The other day I sat down with my daughter, now five, and showed her all the video, pictures and stories we have archived about her and her brother. She loved it, and it was a great way to relive memories.

—JWAIII
ATLANTA, GEORGIA
🐠5 👁2

· · · · · · · ·

FAMILIES WITH WORKING HUSBANDS and stay-at-home moms (or vice versa) should anticipate the following situation after the baby is born. When the husband comes home, he is thinking: "I just worked a full day, and I can't wait to sit down, open a beer, and put up my feet." The wife, on the other hand, is thinking: "I just spent a whole day taking care of this baby; I cannot wait until my husband gets home. I will be standing there with this baby to place in his arms." Anticipate this situation, and plan to deal with it.

–TED RINEY
DALLAS, TEXAS

CELL PHONES CAN BE A REAL LIFELINE to adult contact. I loved talking to friends while I was pushing the stroller when he was just a baby. And I figured if I wasn't on the phone, we would just be walking along in silence. So at least this way he was hearing my voice.

—K.C.
SAN FRANCISCO, CALIFORNIA
😊2

· · · · · · · · ·

If you're moody, talk about it with your hus- band. The more you talk, the more he'll understand.

—TICIA
SYRACUSE,
NEW YORK
😊6 😊4

I LEFT MY SON WITH A BABYSITTER for the first time when he was ten weeks old. But I took him with me to her home for two weeks before I left him alone with her. I thought this would help him form a bond with the babysitter, and it did. It's a good way to get your child acquainted with your babysitter.

—MELANIE WILLIAMS
ATLANTA, GEORGIA
😊4

· · · · · · · · ·

I LEARNED NOT TO LET CHILDREN under the age of one fool me with their small size. They are much smarter and quicker than their size. When my daughter started crawling, which was about six months, she found my video recorder on top of the table, pushed the record button, and started panning the camera around the kitchen. I was shocked that she knew how to handle equipment.

—NORRIS THOMPSON
CHICAGO HEIGHTS, ILLINOIS
😊14 🙈17 🙈8

WE'VE FOUND GREAT BABYSITTERS by putting up flyers in the education department at our local university. Those halls are packed with students who like kids and who need child-care experience.

—MARY
CINCINNATI, OHIO
🍼1 👶14 👶10 👶6

. . . .

If you have to go back to work, do it gradually, if you can. You need time to wean yourself from the baby, not just the other way around.

—JENI L. MORRIS
FLORISSANT, MISSOURI
👶6 👶5 👶3

. . . .

THE TOUGHEST THING I had to do during the first year was leave my daughter and go back to work. I dealt with it because that's what I had to do. But I would call the babysitter a lot and get off from work early when I could.

—REBECCA JEAN GOINS
COLUMBUS, OHIO
👶33 👶20

I FELT SO MUCH MORE SECURE when I went to work knowing that my sons were being taken care of by family. My aunt babysat both of my kids.

—AUDRIANNA JOHNSON
CONYERS, GEORGIA
2 1

My husband takes care of the house so it doesn't look like a bomb went off, and I'm more involved with our baby. Our load is balanced right now.

—M. DeJong
FAIRFAX,
CALIFORNIA
5w

IT WAS SO HARD TO LEAVE MY DAUGHTER and go back to work. I had to leave her with strangers and I called all day long. The lady finally said to me, "The baby is just fine! If she could talk, she would tell you that!"

—LILLIE MARIE CUTTER
STONE MOUNTAIN, GEORGIA
37 24 22

WHEN I STARTED LOOKING FOR BABYSITTERS, I searched on the Web for all the registered sex offenders in my zip-code and surrounding area. I found about 200 sex offenders, with their addresses. I printed out the seven-page sheet and kept it in my purse. One potential babysitter knew three of the sex offenders, and was friends with one of him. After telling her that I didn't feel comfortable with that situation, she said I was being judgmental. But when you have a child, their safety comes first.

—LINDA STOVALL
WESTCHESTER, ILLINOIS
5

I WENT BACK TO WORK TOO SOON. I allowed my sister to watch him within two weeks of having him, but every five minutes I'd call home to check up on him. One time, I called and there was no answer. I thought something bad had happened, so I left work early. When I got home, my sister and my son were asleep. When I asked her why she didn't answer the phone, she just said that she pulled the phone jack out because she was tired of my calling. After that, I decided to take an extra three weeks of unpaid leave; I wasn't ready to be away from my first child.

—DANIELLE CAMRILLO
CHICAGO, ILLINOIS
13 8

· · · · · · · ·

Remember that babies grow up really fast, and while there may be other things you want to accomplish during the day, you only have so much time to enjoy them when they're little.

—BETSY
CINCINNATT, OHIO
5 1 3

I DON'T KNOW HOW I WOULD DO IT without a flexible work arrangement. *Not* having to get up and out of the house two days a week, and *not* having to get him up and dressed and out the door, makes me able to do it on the other days. Ask about flexitime, even if it's just one day a week. It makes a huge difference.

—CAROLE
NEW YORK, NEW YORK
👶2

• • • • • • • •

THE HARDEST PART OF THE FIRST FEW MONTHS for me were when they ended. When Amelia was born, I was on this emotional high for months, and the adrenaline and euphoria I felt kept me going strong. But when it was finally time for us to get out of our little cocoon and for me to get back in the real world, I had a major crash, and was too exhausted to do anything!

—ELIZABETH STOUT
CINCINNATI, OHIO
👶 3

• • • • • • • •

TO HELP ME GET MY LIFE BACK, I had to find a way to get together with adult friends and not talk about babies. I started a mom's group where we talk about world issues, to keep our brains active.

—KATRINA CURRIER
SAN FRANCISCO, CALIFORNIA
👶17M

Getting Out: Entertainment & Trips

The time will come when you are ready to be away from your baby for at least a few hours. This may happen in the first month, or not until your baby is six months old or more. But in anticipation of a grand day or night out, develop a group of reliable, trustworthy babysitters. Grandparents, uncles, aunts, church groups, and neighborhood teens are often good sources. During your first contact with new sitters, hang around to establish a rapport and to observe how they interact with your baby. When you are comfortable, grab the car keys and run. Enjoy an uninterrupted meal, a walk in the park, or a movie. Leave your cell phone number, but try not to call home every ten minutes. Soon you, your baby, and your sitter will enjoy these outings. A good way to ensure your peace of mind is to leave a list of important phone numbers (with yours on top). Written instructions for the sitter could include your "Crying Causes List" (see page 142), feeding and changing hints, and anything else you think they need to know.

You'll gradually get back to your normal life, increasing your activities to longer visits with friends, shopping trips, and other enjoyable activities. But don't expect your life to ever be the same as it was pre-baby. Your priorities will have changed (usually for the better), and your baby will be the center of your existence.

INTRODUCE YOUR CHILD TO MUSIC RIGHT AWAY. As a baby, my oldest child was colicky, so I got a CD player for her early on to soothe her. It helped a little, but the real benefit from that early exposure to music is that now she's a singer and a dancer; she absolutely loves music.

—TINA SMITH
FORT COLLINS, COLORADO
4   2

· · · · · · · · ·

WHEN GOING SOMEWHERE WITH BABY, find the priority entrance. Most museums, restaurants, etc., have a priority entrance so people with special needs and babies don't have to wait in line. Find it and use it! It will make your life so much easier.

—L.C.
PITTSBURGH, PENNSYLVANIA
6   5

· · · · · · · · ·

IT'S NOT WORTH TRYING TO TEACH a baby to play well with other children. They simply don't have the capacity to understand concepts like taking turns or sharing till they're toddlers, and even then it's tough. Just let them play near other kids and keep them from killing each other. Our kids turned out great that way, and now that they're older, they play just fine with others, despite the lack of early training.

—STEPH D.
BALTIMORE, MARYLAND
18   15   13

Blow bubbles in the bathtub. If you spill, it doesn't matter.

—ELIZABETH
FORT COLLINS,
COLORADO

WE HAVE A TAPE THAT'S BEEN PLAYING NON-STOP in the car's cassette player for two years. I think it's called something like, "The Best of Head, Shoulders, Knees and Toes." That falsetto kid won't shut up. He's on every song and for a climax he brings in the rest of the helium gang—just wonderful.

—B.P.
ORLANDO, FLORIDA
21M 7M

. . . .

Give your kids lots of baths. They're not just for cleaning. Kids love to play with water. It provides them with fun and relaxation.

—MEGAN
FORT COLLINS, COLORADO
3 9M

. . . .

OUR SON OFTEN FALLS ASLEEP IN THE CAR, so it makes traveling by car easy. The down side of that, though, is that he sleeps the whole drive and the moment we get to our destination he's ready to go, whether we are or not!

—ROBYN
BIGLERVILLE, PENNSYLVANIA
1

A FEW YEARS AGO, I WAS ON THE HIGHWAY when there was a car accident down the road that backed up traffic for miles. I sat in that car for several hours. It was such a long time I fell asleep. Now that I have kids, I think back to that day and wonder what I would have done if they had been in the car with me. That's why everywhere I go, even if it's only a few miles away, I bring snacks to eat and water to drink. Just in case!

—ANGELA
BETHLEHEM, PENNSYLVANIA
👶5 👶-👶5w

• • • • • • • • •

TRY TO HAVE MIXED-GENDER PLAYGROUPS for your little babies and toddlers. They start to play differently later on, and it's harder to have boys and girls together, but when they're really young, they can play very well with kids of the opposite sex and I think it helped my daughter be comfortable around boys as she was growing up.

—N. CLARK
HOUSTON, TEXAS
👶15

• • • • • • • • •

HIDE AND SEEK IS THE CLASSIC. That, and peek-a-boo with a blanket. Both my kids live for hide and seek. Kids love looking for you and screaming like crazy when they suddenly find you.

—DAVID E. LISS
PENNINGTON, NEW JERSEY
👶4 👶1

*Take them
to the park.
That's how
you wear
them out!*

TABITHA MOTT
CHEYENNE,
WYOMING
👶10 👶7
👶5.5M

JUST DO IT!

IT IS SCARY TAKING YOUR NEWBORN OUT. I worried—do I have everything I need? What if he screams in public? What if I have to nurse? Don't all these idiots on the road realize I am carrying precious cargo in this car? Slow down!

But you have to get out, get over the fears, get used to being in public with your little one. It will do you a world of good and make you proud that you are able to go it alone with just your newborn to that grocery store! What an accomplishment!

—SHEENA KROCK
KUNKLETOWN, PENNSYLVANIA
👶14M

• • • • • • • • •

TAKE YOUR CHILD WITH YOU when you go places. From the beginning, from those first weeks, we took our daughter with us everywhere. Now she's very relaxed when we all go out. She is very used to it. She's not fussy at all.

—APRIL
FORT COLLINS, COLORADO
👶5M

GO TO MUSEUMS WHEN THEY ARE INFANTS, because you won't be able to go later. Once they are toddlers, stick to the playground. Camping is great, but not until they are over one year old. The beach is great anytime. The beach makes the best all-around family vacation.

—JESSICA VAUGHAN
RANDOLPH, VERMONT
10 8 6 4

. . . .

Rather than just sitting at home with my son on weekends, where he can sometimes be fussy, I usually take him on errands. To him a trip to the hardware store is one big adventure.

—JON
BIGLERVILLE, PENNSYLVANIA
1

. . . .

WHAT HELPS ME THE MOST IS TO HAVE SOMEONE with me when I go somewhere, to have that extra set of eyes to help me watch my kids. I usually ask my good friend or my children's grandma to come along on outings.

—JESSICA
MILLIKEN, COLORADO
2 3M

Having babies didn't seem to stop our vacations. We took our babies just about anywhere. Maybe that's why my girls like to travel to this day!

—*Dee*
Oak Lawn,
Illinois
29
24

As soon as you think your baby is ready for it you should arrange a play-date with a friend's or relative's young child. It really helps a child's development to interact with children their own age. They can learn to share and work together to solve little problems and challenges. It is especially important if your child is an only child.

—Don Rodgers
North Huntingdon, Pennsylvania
17 14

• • • • • • • •

I joined Mothers & More (a national organization with local chapters, http://www.mothersandmore.org) to socialize with other moms and have my son participate in playgroups. They have something similar to a babysitting co-op. I watch another member's child one night and she will watch mine another night, free of charge. My son is in trusted hands and gets to play with a familiar friend.

—Leslie Bundy
Waukesha, Wisconsin
1

• • • • • • • •

I participated in a playgroup to provide my child with an "extended family." The great thing was having a support group of parents. Plus, no matter what age or stage my child was at, there was always somebody else in the group who had been through it already.

—Dona Lessin
New York, New York
32

I SEE SO MANY PARENTS TAKE THEIR KIDS places with no
toys to play with and then wonder why their kids act up!
Even when my daughter was a baby, I kept a big basket
of toys in the car at all times. Then when we needed to
go someplace, such as to a friend's house or a doctor's office, I'd haul the basket inside. Friends com-
ment on how well-behaved and well-entertained
Rachel always is. It's so simple: I think it's because she
always has something to keep her occupied.

—CAROL GILMORE
EASTON, PENNSYLVANIA
6

. . . .

Playgrounds for only a few minutes are almost worse than no playgrounds at all.

—S.S.
DALY CITY, CALIFORNIA
4   1

. . . .

JOIN A PLAYGROUP! It helps keep you sane. I really enjoy
both aspects of being part of a playgroup. I'm a stay-at-
home mom, so my children normally wouldn't get much
social interaction. But they get to make friends in a playgroup. And I really appreciate the other parents in the
group. We can gab and cry on each other's shoulders!

—MELISSA GROOM
FORT COLLINS, COLORADO
2   5M

KEEP THE TV OUT OF YOUR HOUSE. Never use the TV as a de facto babysitter while dinner is being made or whatever. Increased TV watching is proportional to increased behavioral issues. Kids create a richer imaginary life when you turn them toward books.

—ANONYMOUS
BETHESDA, MARYLAND
9 6

We dressed our five kids alike when we traveled, so that if one got lost, we could point to the others and say, 'He looks just like him . . . only smaller.'

—ELAINE FANTLE SHIMBERG
TAMPA, FLORIDA
41 40 38 37 32

LATHER YOURSELF AND YOUR BABY with sunscreen (careful near the eyes), plop on floppy hats, and go out and play! Sure, the housework needs to be done, but it can wait. Even if you're drained, a trip to the park will perk you up . . . and maybe even help your baby take a nice, long nap afterwards.

—GRACIELA SHOLANDER
FORT COLLINS, COLORADO
12 10

I HAD MY DAUGHTER HELP ASSEMBLE an Adirondack chair with me when she was 14 months old. She handed me the screws and felt like she was helping. We painted a room together too. She made an absolute mess but she really felt like she was a part of it. Having her help allows me to get things done, and usually the mess cleans up easily.

> —NANCY
> PORTLAND, MAINE
> 🙊2

• • • • • • • •

THE MOMENT I TOOK MY SON OUTSIDE, whether it was snowing or sunny, he was happy as can be. I recommend that you get out as much as you can—nurse outside, attach the baby jumper to a tree, take a portable cradlette. I loved to put my son in a carrier on my back, put on my snowshoes and go outside for a walk.

> —JENNIFER TAYLOR ATANDA
> ALEXANDRIA, VIRGINIA
> 😊2

• • • • • • • •

KIDS LOVE TO SHARE YOUR interests with you, and you should make time to be with them, even if it's when you're performing household tasks. I built a swing set for my son. At age one year and nine months, he was my key helper.

> —BILL
> BOSTON, MASSACHUSETTS
> 😊-🙊2

Make sure you have an extra set of clothes in the car for your kids, because they always get dirty.

—VERONICA
LOVELAND,
COLORADO
😊4 🙊3
😊1

GO OUTSIDE AND PLAY! I think it's really important for mom and baby to get out and talk with other moms and kids and socialize. We live close to the park and we walk there every day. Sometimes we sit and watch the geese and ducks on the pond.

—SUZANNE NAYDUCH
FORT COLLINS, COLORADO
8M

Get down on the floor and play with your kid. Think like a kid. Move like a kid. Adjust your life to be more in tune with your kid.

—BRITT STROMBERG
CAMANO ISLAND, WASHINGTON
11M

• • • • • • • •

DON'T FEEL LIKE YOU HAVE TO MOVE to the suburbs to raise kids. I love having urban kids. I don't have to drive much, which means a lot less hassle getting them in and out of the car. We just get in the stroller and off we go! And there is so much to do with them—museums with activities for kids, huge parks and playgrounds, and mommy groups. It keeps life more interesting for me as a stay-at-home mom, too!

—RACHEL B.
PHILADELPHIA, PENNSYLVANIA
3 2

• • • • • • • •

WHEN MY DAUGHTER WAS REALLY LITTLE she liked watching birds, so we'd go to a local bookstore with a big window where we could watch them. They'd flap their wings and she'd giggle in hysterics.

—TALLIE FISHBURNE
MINNEAPOLIS, MINNESOTA
14M

WHENEVER YOU LEAVE THE HOUSE with kids, pack a snack to take with you wherever you go. Cheerios and animal crackers work well. And when I have enough time to think ahead, I pack cut up vegetables.

—J. McNally
LOVELAND, COLORADO
9 7 16M

WE THOUGHT IT WOULD BE GREAT to take our son to the zoo when he was six months old, but he was too young to be engaged or even interested. We stood in front of this elephant for 15 minutes, while he looked down at a patch of dirt on the ground.

—R.Q.
SAN FRANCISCO, CALIFORNIA
6M

Never be afraid to do things with your family. Buy backpacks and a bike trailer —you can take your kids with you anywhere.

—NICOLE DAVIS
RACHO CORDOVA
10 5
2

PEOPLE THINK THEY NEED TO ENTERTAIN their kids constantly. Don't! I remember having babies and toddlers who were just so content to sit on a floor with a simple toy or a book or paper and crayons or even just some cardboard, and they would play for a long time. They learned how to use their imaginations and entertain themselves. Those are valuable skills.

—MATT W.
SAN CARLOS, CALIFORNIA
24 22 19

DON'T "DUMB IT DOWN" FOR YOUR CHILDREN. My one-year-old son loves the music that my husband and I listen to—salsa and jazz—and when we're driving he loves the classic R&B radio station. Kiddie music does not appeal to him.

—C.C.
SAN FRANCISCO, CALIFORNIA
👶1

* * * * * * * *

IT'S NEVER TOO EARLY TO SIGN up for exercise classes with your babies. At three months, children can start something like a "Music Together" program. My Mommy & Me class offers stretching and low-impact aerobics, using exercise bands. Classes organized through the city or community centers are great; they provide socialization before the kids begin pre-school—and, it's motivating to be with other mothers.

—T.N.
HUNTINGTON BEACH, CALIFORNIA
👩19M 👶3.5M

* * * * * * * *

RIGHT FROM THE BEGINNING, OUR LITTLE GUY loved music and by 16 months he could identify all four Beatles! We listen to all kinds of music with him and get a kick out of how fast he'll say, "Not that one," after just a few notes. It's like "Name That Tune" with a toddler!

—CHRISTINE BEIDEL
RUTHERFORD, NEW JERSEY
👩11 👶2

Be prepared for anything. Always have an extra set of clothes, a camera for all those "firsts," snacks, diaper wipes, and a first aid kit.

—JESSICA
MILLIKEN,
COLORADO
👶2 👩3M

CHILD'S PLAY

A SIMPLE RASPBERRY—OR BRONX CHEER, as it once was called—will make a child smile as easily (and much more cheaply) than any toy. Bouncing a baby on my knees, walking her under the bow of a leafing tree, exploring the cats' toes—it all delighted her more, much more, than some huge plastic thing that whirls and gongs and whizzes.

—MARION ROACH
TROY, NEW YORK

• • • • • • • •

OUR DAUGHTER THOUGHT IT WAS A RIOT WHEN I DROPPED a towel on her and covered her up after her bath. We would do this over and over, with her laughter cracking me up. It was totally ridiculous and so much fun.

—NANCY ENGLISH
PORTLAND, MAINE

• • • • • • • •

PLAY WITH YOUR BABY. It's important for you and the baby. It makes you both laugh and you can learn from the baby how to be more spontaneous and have more fun. Shake your head in a silly way, stick out your tongue, cross your eyes—babies really appreciate simple games like that.

—S.C.
HELOTES, TEXAS
30

WE'VE TAKEN OUR THREE-YEAR-OLD on at least 20 round trip flights, and our one-year-old on about eight. We've hardly found it worthwhile to buy an extra seat for the kid, since they hardly napped and won't stay there when they can be on your lap or eating peanuts off the floor. Also, you can just bring a car seat on the plane and hope you get lucky with an extra seat; even if there are not continuous seats, people will be more than happy to get out of your way so they don't end up next to a baby. For entertainment, kids are absolutely fascinated by the barf bag, flight safety card, and plastic cups (ask for an extra one). If that fails to amuse them, try bribery—our three-year-old gets M&Ms if she's good on the flight.

—MARK KAPLAN
FOSTER CITY, CALIFORNIA
3 1

* * * * * * * *

Please, never take a baby out to eat.

*—ANONYMOUS
MONTCLAIR,
NEW JERSEY*

WHEN MY HUSBAND AND I WERE PLANNING our vacation to Venice, Italy, we didn't prepare for traveling with a baby. We packed everything we would need for the baby, but Venice is not a stroller-friendly city—mostly because you need to take small boats to get around and strollers did not work well in the boats. To make it worse, I brought the big stroller because I thought that the baby would be more comfortable. He was more comfortable. But we were limited in what we could do and where we could go.

—LORAINE BRANCATTO BOERSMA
TOLEDO, OHIO
6 4

WHEN GOING ON A FAMILY VACATION, definitely get the kids loaded up with lots of activities—coloring and activity books, even a mini-walkman to listen to music. We play the alphabet game—you call out the letters on the road signs from "A" to "Z"—and other games like that.

—K.J.
ST. AUGUSTINE, FLORIDA
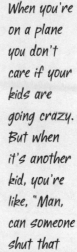 6 1

. . . .

MY BABY HATED BEING CONFINED to her carseat, and she would become so hysterical that I would have to pull over many times to get out and comfort her. I learned that when traveling a long distance, I should plan for someone to come with me to sit with her and distract her. Lots of snacks and toys help too.

—PAULA FOX
GORHAM, MAINE
2

. . . .

IT'S EASIER TO TAKE A ROAD TRIP WITH A BABY if you put them in the car at their bedtime and drive through the night. That way, he or she can sleep during the ride and you can concentrate on driving. We did this on a trip from Philadelphia to Iowa and it worked perfectly. The next time, we drove during the day and it was a rough ride.

—RICK
NARBERTH, PENNSYLVANIA
4M

When you're on a plane you don't care if your kids are going crazy. But when it's another kid, you're like, "Man, can someone shut that kid up?"

—EDDIE
FINKELSTEIN
CHAPPAQUA,
NEW YORK
16 14
9

SING IT LOUD

Sing to your baby. Babies love music. Singing is very soothing. I have to do that a lot as a nanny with the twins I take care of. If they're both crying, I can't take care of both of them at the same time. When I'm trying to get them ready to eat, they're usually both crying as I'm mixing up their cereal. They start listening to me singing and they forget their troubles a little bit.

If they're fussing while I'm feeding them and having a hard time accepting the food, the singing always seems to work. The song they like at the moment is, "The Wheels On the Bus."

I try to be animated when I sing. I dance around the room a little bit. The motion gets their attention. They stop dead in their tracks like they've seen a ghost and stare at me. Then, they smile because they're like, "Oh, I kind of like this song." If there's an older child, have him or her help. I'll say, "Do a dance for the baby."

—Debbie L.
Camillus, New York
12

I ALWAYS TALKED TO THE BABIES and babbled away at them about whatever I was doing or thinking. I think that communication is really important, even when the baby can't understand.

—BRETTE SEMBER
CLARENCE, NEW YORK
👶12 👶6

• • • • • • • •

DON'T MAKE THE MISTAKE OF TRAVELING through the night when your baby sleeps. If you do, when the day comes, you won't have gotten any sleep but your baby will be wide awake and ready to go. I've seen lots of people try this, and they just get frustrated. Instead, we leave around six a.m. and stop driving for the day around four p.m. It works very well.

—STACY MCHARGUE
SAN ANTONIO, TEXAS
👶12 👶11

• • • • • • • •

AIR TRAVEL WITH A BABY IS A BREEZE. Strollers can be checked at the gate and when the plane lands, you get it right back. Also, a lot of car rental places let you check out car seats so you don't have to bring your own. When we travel we look for places that rent child-friendly equipment, like beach joggers. Usually you can get what you need delivered right to your door.

—STEPHANIE
WINDSOR, COLORADO
👶2 👶7M

We bought a DVD player with an LCD screen for the car. We stick it on the back of the seat for the kids. It's great for road trips.

—TAMI MEYERS
FORT COLLINS, COLORADO
👶11 👶7
👶4

REMEMBER THAT A BABY HAS AS MUCH RIGHT to be on a plane as that cranky, child-less business traveler who thinks the world revolves around him or her. Sure, the baby disrupts the flight with screaming, fussing, uncontainable laughter, playing patty cake with the head of the person in front of them. But the cranky, child-less business traveler disrupts the flight with rude stares, loud and selfish complaints, and bad karma. And they won't even hold your kid for one minute while you clean up the puke on the floor. Personally, I don't think cranky, child-less business travelers should be allowed on planes. They can't handle the tight, stressful quarters for such long periods of time. But unless the airlines change the rules, I won't make an issue out of it.

—JWAIII
ATLANTA, GEORGIA
👧5 👶2

• • • • • • • • •

Go to Club Med. They have the best vacations if you have a baby.

—L.C.
PITTSBURGH,
PENNSYLVANIA
👶6 👧5

BEFORE YOU TRAVEL WITH A BABY on a bus, train, or plane, take a six-foot-long piece of parachute cord (or other strong cord) and tie four or five toys to it. This way, when your kid tries to throw the toys, they don't go far, and you won't spend half of your journey crawling on the floor trying to retrieve them. (Of course, this is not for unattended play, but it should be perfectly safe while you're sitting right beside your baby.)

—JEAN NICK
KINTNERSVILLE, PENNSYLVANIA
👧16 👶14

THE WORST TRIP I EVER TOOK was a visit my sister's with my eight-month-old daughter. I'd just flown in with her from across the country. My parent's picked us up, but they had failed to get the carseat properly installed. It took us over an hour to fix it. By the time we were driving, it was exactly the wrong time for my daughter, who'd been trapped on various moving vehicles all day. She screamed her head off for the whole two hours.

—JENNY W.
NEW YORK, NEW YORK
🐶4

. . . .

IF YOU'RE FLYING WITH AN INFANT, make sure the baby is drinking from a bottle on the way up and on the way down. This keeps the ears open and the child from crying due to ears hurting from the change in altitude. And a change of clothes is a must, along with a travel stroller that allows you to wheel the baby right up to your seat.

—JANE COVNER
SHERMAN OAKS, CALIFORNIA
😊18

. . . .

I LOVE TRYING TO MAKE MY DAUGHTER LAUGH and trying to entertain her. Of course it usually only lasts about 15 minutes before she loses interest.

—JOHN D. CALLEY
ALEXANDRIA, VIRGINIA
🐶4M

Don't be afraid to take the baby to restaurants in the very beginning. When they are infants there's a great window of opportunity to get out without much fuss.

—RUSS COX
PORTLAND,
MAINE
🐶-🐶5
😊1

TRAVELING WITH A BABY IS EASY. They mostly sleep on plane and car trips because there is nothing else to do.

—ANONYMOUS
GOLDEN, COLORADO
👶15M

IT IS AN UNMITIGATED PAIN, BUT ALSO WORTH IT to lug car seats onto the airplane for trips of any considerable distance. We did it and while we could have lived without the angry stares from other passengers—especially when a flight attendant had to order the pilot to stop the plane as we taxied toward takeoff so one of the car seats could be moved to the aisle seat—it allowed both our children to snooze peacefully almost the entire two-plus hour flight. Plus, we knew the kids were safe when we put them in our rental car.

—KEITH REGAN
GRAFTON, MASSACHUSETTS
👶5 👶3

NEVER TRAVEL ON AN AIRPLANE with a baby. You've got to take the car seat and when they are awake, everyone's awake. We took my son at 10 months. He was starting to walk, so he wanted to be able to move around and crawl but couldn't. And you know, there is soooooo much space on an airplane to change a diaper.

—WESLEY ANDERSON
SAN ANTONIO, TEXAS
👶2

GETTING SOME AIR ... SAFELY

After the first few months there will be times when you want to take your baby with you on outings to visit friends, grandparents or other relatives or just to get out for a walk. It's good for you and good for the baby, but careful planning is essential. Most important, your car seat must be properly installed. (often there are clinics to insure safe installation run by pediatric hospitals, or police or fire departments). Your baby should be rear-facing and in the middle of the back seat. Don't plan to take your baby on trips where he or she will be exposed to numerous people; some of them will have a contagious disease, which they might share with your child as they are admiring her. For the first few car trips, especially on a journey of more than a half-hour, it's a good idea to have someone with you, beside the baby, so that distractions to your driving will be kept to a minimum.

THE FIRST TIME WE FLEW WITH OUR DAUGHTER, she stayed on my wife's lap. The woman who sat in front of them was wearing a big black hat with tons of these little colorful pins all over it. The pins had little cars, little teddy bears, little toys, hanging off them. Our daughter's eyes lit up. She lunged for the hat as I held her back with all I had in me. The rest of the flight (we hadn't even taxied down the runway yet) is gone from my memory.

—DAVID LISS
PENNINGTON, NEW JERSEY
4 1

When we take car trips, the key is to listen to Sesame Street CDs on the ride. It calms and entertains my daughter and she doesn't scream the whole way.

—RUSSELL LISSAU
ARLINGTON HEIGHTS, ILLINOIS
2

I JUST TRAVELED WITH MY 15-MONTH-OLD SON from Tanzania without my wife because we couldn't get on the same flight. The plane ride was 17 hours and it was the first time I had spent more than one or two hours alone with him. Changing diapers on the plane was difficult and there were times when my son was crying and I did not know what to do. But I cherished the experience.

—M.Z. NAAB
ARLINGTON, VIRGINIA
15M

WHENEVER YOU GO TO A WEDDING, funeral, church service or some special event with your baby, always sit near the back for an easy getaway.

—ANDREA PARKER
CHICAGO, ILLINOIS
5

An Apple a Day: Health & Growth Issues

t's probable that you already met your chosen pediatrician at a prenatal visit or in the hospital where the baby was born. She or he will let you know when you should bring in your new baby for the first well-baby visit. At that time, growth and development will be evaluated, along with a physical examination.

In most states, a blood test will have been done in the hospital prior to discharge. The blood is usually taken from the foot and sent for a PKU test. This test checks for much more than PKU (which is a rare form of metabolic disorder, best diagnosed with this early blood test. It enables your pediatrician to treat your baby and avoid symptoms of the disease using a special diet.) Many other rare metabolic diseases will also be ruled out by this test. It is often repeated at an early well-child visit.

New parents should make a list of questions and concerns to discuss with the pediatrician at every well-child visit. Concerns about growth, development, nutrition, visitors, fluoride needs in your area, and much more are all appropriate at each visit. There will be many other questions you will think of between visits; add them to the list. It's always helpful when both parents can attend well-child visits.

If routine immunizations have not already been started, they will be. Make sure your baby gets all recommended immunizations at each visit. The number of injections can be distressing, but all are important and should be given according to your pediatrician's suggested schedule. There are more and more combination vaccines available, which may decrease the number of injections your baby and you will have to endure.

BABIES CAN FIND WAYS TO GET THEMSELVES into mischief, so you have to think ahead. If there is something that you are not sure is secure, then secure it.

—MARIA
EAST PALESTINE, OHIO
👶18 👧16 👶12

• • • • • • • •

DON'T BE AFRAID TO CALL the doctor if you think there is a problem, even a minor one. Most first-time parents feel that people will think they are overreacting if they call for help every time the baby sneezes, but I've always said I'd rather be safe than sorry.

—JIM R.
NEGLEY, OHIO
👧15

• • • • • • • •

You don't know what it means to be a parent until your baby starts to crawl.

—JWAIII
ATLANTA,
GEORGIA
👧5 👶2

WHEN MY FIRST CHILD TURNED TWO, I introduced him to the world of chocolate. I gave him one small piece, but he wanted more. So I thought, "Why not?" and gave him a couple more pieces. I inadvertently left the chocolate bar in a place too accessible to his little hands. Within a second of me turning my head, he had stuffed an entire bar into his mouth, wrapping and all. I was terrified that he was going to start choking, but he wolfed down every-thing and sat there with a look on his face that said, "More." Of course, later that day he was sick as a dog.

—BILLIE
NEW YORK, NEW YORK
👶5 👧18M

I HAD ALWAYS LEFT MY BABY ON THE SOFA, with a soft ottoman pulled in tight, and she was always safe and fine. One day, before I even knew she could really crawl, I was in another room and I heard this thump. I ran in and of course she had scooted herself off the edge of the sofa. Luckily, she wasn't really hurt, but I finally believed it when people warned me not to leave a child on sofas, chairs, or other "high" places!

—K. JONES
PHILADELPHIA, PENNSYLVANIA
🐵14 👶10 👶6

• • • • • • • •

OUR 14-MONTH-OLD DAUGHTER is a little ball of energy. Once, we were walking out of a Vietnamese restaurant and she went dashing out the door, nearly into traffic. As much as you hear people say it, it holds so true: You have to watch your children at all times. You never know when your child will dart off and find a bottle of Crystal Drano.

—KERRY ROME
HERMOSA BEACH, CALIFORNIA
🐵14M

• • • • • • • •

ENJOY EACH UNIQUE STAGE of your child's development. Some people say, "I can't wait until he gets to walking or talking." As you keep wishing, they'll grow faster and you'll miss things.

—KEN BECKERING
SYRACUSE, NEW YORK
👶5 🐵3

A VERY HELPFUL PHRASE TO TEACH small kids is "come here." This works great if you need to distract your kids to stop them from fighting. It can also be a life-saver if they're doing something dangerous. It's a very positive intervention. Rather than yelling at them, you're simply telling them to "come here."

—TORI DENNIS
IRON CITY, TENNESSEE
👪 8 👪 6 👪 5

* * * * * * * * *

KEEP THE TOLL-FREE POISON EMERGENCY HOTLINE number (1-800-222-1222) near the phone and call immediately if you suspect your child has been in contact with a poison. Even in a "baby-proofed" home, bad things can happen and parents should have no fear of being judged for "allowing" their child to touch/taste/breathe a poison. Calls to a poison center are handled by nurses, pharma-cists and doctors and are completely confidential.

—CHRIS FALK
CHEVY CHASE, MARYLAND
👶 4 👶 1.5

* * * * * * * * *

MY SON WOULD EAT LITERALLY ANYTHING. One day, he was munching on something and he grinned at me. His teeth were bright blue! He had bitten off the end of a blue non-toxic marker and sucked it.

—DEBORAH W. YOUNG
LITHONIA, GEORGIA
👶 22 👪 25

AVOID PERMANENT MARKERS LIKE THE PLAGUE. When my daughter was around two, we had just had the house painted and she saw the electrical outlet in the wall, which had no plastic plugs. She saw the two little vertical lines with the little hole and thought it looked like a bunny rabbit's face. With a permanent marker, she drew the ears of the bunny to go with it. It wasn't dangerous, but it was maddening and hilarious.

—NAOMI NEMTZOW
BROOKLYN, NEW YORK
22 -15

· · · · · · · · ·

BEFORE THE CHILDREN CAN CRAWL, remove all CDs from the premises. Every single one of them is a meal waiting to be eaten, as well as a little book (you know, the liner notes) waiting to be ripped or chewed to shreds. I'm not saying I have to replace my entire CD collection. Just about a third of it.

—DAVID E. LISS
PENNINGTON, NEW JERSEY
4 1

· · · · · · · · ·

I'D PARKED THE CAR AT THE MALL, and it was really hot outside. When I returned and put my son back in his car seat, his arm got burned; part of the car that he touched had been exposed to the sun.

—DYLETTE DAVIS
FULLERTON, CALIFORNIA
16

USE A SPECIAL WORD TO GET THEIR ATTENTION quickly.
Instead of always saying "No," or "Don't do that," we
have two special words that we use for situations when we
want our daughter to stop quickly. The first word is "danger." We say "Danger!" to prevent her from getting hurt,
as in "Don't run into the street," or "Don't climb on top of
the cabinets." The second word is "ugly." We use this one
to stop behavior that's not nice, like hitting or pushing.

—SHARI LONG, CNM (MIDWIFE)
CHEYENNE, WYOMING
👶21 👶19 👶12 👶2

• • • • • • • •

MY HUSBAND AND I HAVE MADE lots of mistakes since
bringing our baby home. We've knocked his head into
doorways, dropped a couple of things on his head, and
spilled food on him. Fortunately, none of our mistakes
made him cry, so we assume and hope we didn't hurt him.

—ANONYMOUS
MINNEAPOLIS, MINNESOTA
👶1

INFANT INFO

Having a dog around the house during your baby's
first year of life may lead to a reduction in allergies as
he or she grows older.

AFTER MY GRANDSON STARTED TO CRAWL, my daughter literally crawled all around the house so she could see from a baby's perspective what he could get into, hurt himself with, etc.

—NOLA SMITH
TAMPA, FLORIDA
41 35

* * * * * * * *

Fathers should not try to hold a sick baby above their shoulders. And mothers should not laugh when he gets puked on.

—D.R.
SYRACUSE, NEW YORK
8 4 16M

* * * * * * * *

BRONCHITIS CAN BE EASILY CURED! My son constantly gets attacks of bronchitis after a cold. The doctors gave him antibiotics, which helped, but also gave him diarrhea. Now, I place a steamer in his room. Sometimes, I put a drop of eucalyptus in the steamer, but often plain water is enough. The steam loosens the phlegm so he can cough it up more easily. Within a day or two, the bronchitis is all gone—without using antibiotics!

—BEATRICE
MIAMI, FLORIDA

HAVE AN EMERGENCY NUMBER HANDY. One night, my nine-month-old daughter started choking on bread. I was terrified. I didn't know what to do to stop the choking so I called the emergency number. The operator told me that, since she was not turning blue, she was still getting air. They instructed me to give her some water to wash it down. It worked! Thankfully, they stayed on the phone with me until she stopped choking and was breathing normally. The whole event lasted only about two minutes, but it was the scariest two minutes of my life.

—F.T.L.
METZ, FRANCE
5 3

· · · · · · · ·

WITH MY SONS, I WAS TOO PROTECTIVE. I was always shielding them, trying to keep them close. I have a totally different perspective with my fourth child, who's my only daughter. I expose her to many different situations and people, and as a result she's happy, outgoing, and joyful.

—SHARI LONG, CNM (MIDWIFE)
CHEYENNE, WYOMING
21 19 12 2

· · · · · · · ·

BUY AHEAD. GET CLOTHES at the end of a season for the size your kid will be next year. You'll save tons of money!

—J.D.
BALTIMORE, MARYLAND
15 3

BABY FOOD . . . MMM, GOOD

MAKE YOUR OWN BABY FOOD! I know that many people feel they don't have the time—especially with everything else you're doing every day for baby. I was reluctant, too. But it is so easy and quick. And it's much healthier than buying it. I made my own baby food without using a blender. Just ask your friends if you can have their Gerber jars so you can put your own food in them.

—NANCY
BRUSSELS, BELGIUM

• • • • • • • • •

HAVE YOU EVER TASTED STORE-BOUGHT BABY FOOD? It's terrible. When my daughter was a baby, I vowed that I wouldn't feed her anything that I wouldn't eat myself. Instead, I pureed some of the food that my husband and I were eating and fed it to her. It worked great, especially with carrots, peas, and sweet potatoes. I'd freeze any leftover puree in ice cube trays. Then if I needed a quick meal for her, it was simple to defrost a cube or two in the microwave for a few seconds.

—CAROL GILMORE
EASTON, PENNSYLVANIA
6

WHEN I WAS IN FRANCE, I NOTICED THE BABIES there ate all sorts of "real" food—not just the usual chicken nuggets and PBJs I was used to seeing kids eat. Somebody there told me the secret was to give babies regular adult food, just pureed. So, when we had our own babies, we gave them pureed "real" food as soon as possible. I have friends who say their kids just wanted milk or rice cereal, but my babies ate lasagna, garlicky pasta salad, stewed veggies, strong cheeses, and even slightly spicy foods. And now they just happily eat whatever we eat!

—J.W.
ROCHESTER, NEW YORK
13

. . . .

FOOD IS TRICKY. Sometimes I go to bed at the end of the day and I wonder, "What did my daughter eat that's healthy?" I just keep offering her good foods, but I don't make special meals just for her. She has to learn to eat what the rest of us eat.

—CHERI
FORT COLLINS, COLORADO
1

I REFUSED TO BUY BABY FOOD. Instead, I ground up my own fresh carrots and green beans, I made homemade yogurt and granola, and I fed my babies breast milk. The natural method saved me money and worked wonders for their health. To this day, they don't get ear infections, and they're lean and trim with tons of energy.

—S.H.
New Lenox, Illinois
25 17 15

• • • • • • • • •

DON'T BE AFRAID TO FEED KIDS A VARIETY of "adult" foods, not just the same old mashed banana baby foods. I had a little blender set up in the kitchen. I would just take whatever we were eating, unless it was something spicy, and blend it up for the babies. They ate well and all grew up to be great eaters.

—Lori T.
Charleston, South Carolina
36 34 31 26

TO KEEP MY CABINET CONTENTS INTACT and still keep my kids safe, I chose the cabinet farthest away from the refrigerator and stove and dedicated it to their stuff. I put all of their dishes and sippy cups in it. My daughter and my son both know that it is their cabinet. Then, when they try to go into other cabinets, I firmly say, "No, that's Mommy's." It's really amazing how well this simple technique works.

—PAULA
NORTHAMPTON, PENNSYLVANIA
3 1

* * * * * * * *

EARLY ON I REALIZED THAT THE ISSUE of clothing was a small battle, not one I was going to engage in. My daughter dislikes any bows, frills, epaulets. She likes sleek, simple things, despises dresses and has no patience for any patterns. And who cares? This is the small stuff. I choose which issues to battle over, and this in not one of them.

—MARION ROACH
TROY, NEW YORK

* * * * * * * *

ONE TIME, WHEN I HAD THE BABY IN MY ARMS, I fell out of my car when my foot got caught in the diaper bag. I fell with my baby in the air —I was holding him in my hands above my head.

—NIKOL
SANTA MONICA, CALIFORNIA
1

MAKE SURE YOU BABY-PROOF THE HOUSE before your kid can crawl, which can happen very suddenly. I left my daughter in her normal play area well before she could crawl and went in the other room for 30 seconds to get socks. When I came back, she had rolled all the way over to a very heavy, breakable, tippy pot we had on the floor. Luckily, both the pot and baby were fine, but another five seconds and it would have been a different story.

—S. COLEMAN
NEW YORK, NEW YORK
8M

. . . .

Sunscreen stick is really handy. It's like Chapstick; it's easy to apply.

—J. MCNALLY
LOVELAND,
COLORADO
9 7
16M

PARENTS WHO HAVE KIDS WITH CHRONIC EAR infections should at least look into the option of ear tubes. Our son had ear infections constantly, starting from about nine months old. We kept bringing him in to the doctor, who'd prescribe us antibiotics, and it would go away for a few weeks. Then it would come back and we'd do it all over again. I really hated giving him so many antibiotics. If I knew then what I know now, I think I would have had them do the surgery to put longer tubes in his ears. I realize the doctors do everything they can to avoid surgery, but I think that taking too many antibiotics is bad for the baby. And the infections were really painful.

—JULIE
SAN FRANCISCO, CALIFORNIA
13

ONE TIME, MY EIGHT-MONTH-OLD SON hit his head four times in one day. The first time, he crawled over my legs and fell on his head. Later, he tumbled out of his crib (we didn't even know he could climb!). The third time, he looked up and hit his head on the bars. The fourth, I was carrying him and dropped something, and when I went to pick it up, I hit his head on the side mirror of my car. I called the doctor's office and I was certain they would call child protective services. But they didn't, and he was fine.

—ANONYMOUS
SAN ANTONIO, TEXAS
👧3 👶1 👦7M

• • • • • • • • •

WHEN MY SON WAS A YEAR AND A HALF OLD, he developed a fever and started acting unusually cranky, so we just assumed he was teething. One day, I went to pick him up at preschool and noticed his ear was incredibly hot and oozing yellow puss. Panicked, I rushed him to the doctor and found out his eardrum had burst while he was sleeping. The symptoms I had attributed to teething actually indicated the early stages of an ear infection, too. I wish I would have known this earlier.

—CHERI HURD
LITTLETON, COLORADO
👧26 👶23 👧21 👦14

MILK: WHAT & WHEN

The AAP recommends that breast-fed babies not be fed solid foods until about six months of age. Bottle-fed babies may start solids between four and six months. The order of introduction of solid foods varies depending on whom you ask and what you read. I have always suggested that the "ugly" foods be introduced first. Cereal is a good first food, and is also fortified with iron, the only thing breast milk may lack. I like to start with rice cereal and then introduce one new food each week. This way, if your baby reacts to a new food, you will know which one it is.

I usually introduce a second pure-grain cereal next (barley), and then yellow veggies (carrots, squash, and sweet potatoes) followed by green vegetables (peas, beans, and spinach). Meats are next (lamb, beef, poultry, and pork), and then the fruits. Remember to stick to the one-new-food-a-week plan.

I don't recommend adding a sweet fruit to a food that is bland (like cereal). A baby's tastes are different than ours and if they get used to the bland foods, the good-tasting foods are easier to introduce.

WHEN YOU SCREW UP, don't get racked with guilt. We all do it. I felt so bad when my baby burned herself on a hot pan I'd left out. When I told people what happened, every parent had a similar story—dropping a kid, dropping something on a kid, burning a kid, forgetting a kid somewhere. People make mistakes. If the baby doesn't come out of the experience with any major injuries, just thank your lucky stars and move on with your life.

—SUSAN
CHICAGO, ILLINOIS
4 1

* * * * * * * *

I WAS LUCKY. MY SISTER-IN-LAW had six kids, plus the people at my church were so tickled when I had twin girls that I didn't have to actually buy clothes until they were a 2T. Then, I basically hit Goodwill Stores or ReUzIt Shops. I still do, even for my oldest.

—JEANNE ECKMAN
LANCASTER, PENNSYLVANIA
11 -5

* * * * * * * *

MY SON HAD AN APPETITE FOR BUGS. We used to joke that we didn't need to call an exterminator. It was pretty gross and I don't even want to think about how many he actually ingested. The good news is he's over that phase and sticks to a diet of mostly healthy food.

—ANONYMOUS
VAN NUYS, CALIFORNIA
2

WHEN MY KIDS GOT TO THE POINT where they wanted to dress themselves, I would try to coordinate everything— shirt, pants, socks, hair bow. But inevitably they'd want to wear their favorite socks or "best shirt" and it usually didn't match anything they had on. One day, my friend told me that if they're doing it themselves, then just deal with it. It may not be perfect, but at least you didn't have to do it. Even if nothing matches, who cares? They're proud that they've done something for themselves. That's all that really matters.

—J.K.
CLIFTON SPRINGS, NEW YORK
11 8

. . . .

MY HUSBAND WAS PLAYING with our daughter, lifting her up and swinging her around. They were laughing when we heard a pop. Our daughter's elbow had popped out of the joint! Because children have such flexible joints, it is easy for this to occur. She was in a lot of pain, but the doctor quickly popped it back into the joint. He advised us to be careful with young children and avoid swinging even during playtime.

—P.
PORTLAND, OREGON

I ALWAYS LOVED TO SEW AND THOUGHT I'd sew all these
adorable little baby clothes. But don't count on it—once
you've got the baby, you'll barely have the time! Plus,
baby clothes are not that expensive nowadays, unless you
get the fancy stuff, and it probably costs more to buy the
fabric than to just buy discount baby clothes.

—JILL H.
NEW YORK, NEW YORK
14 12

* * * * * * * *

DON'T TAKE THE SIZE TAGS ON BABY CLOTHES too literally.
My daughter is 10 months old and wears some sweaters
that say "newborn, 0-3 months," some pants that say "3-
6 months," some sleepers that say "6-9" or "6-12
months," and a hat that says "12-18 months." Sweaters,
especially, seem to run big for some reason.

—K.T.
BURLINGTON, VERMONT
5 4 1

* * * * * * * *

HAND-ME-DOWNS ARE OK FOR BABIES if the clothes are
in good shape. They really won't know the difference.
When they're crawling what's most important is to
get sturdy clothes. And, they just need to be clean.
When they're teething, it's a good idea to have
babies wear a bib. Otherwise, their shirts get wet
and worn when they chew on them.

—PAM BOEA
SYRACUSE, NEW YORK
19 17 -15 12

CLOTHES FOR BABY

I LOVE EBAY! I bought a lot of my son's clothing from eBay and saved a ton! You can get brand new clothing with the tags still attached for next to nothing. You can also get clothing inexpensively by buying it out of season.

—ERIN CALLAHAN
KERSHAW, SOUTH CAROLINA
👶2

. . . .

HAVE A WIDE VARIETY OF SIZES AVAILABLE for the baby. My first weighed 11 ½ pounds and was into three-month size immediately and then soon into six-month size. My second, however, was eight pounds, 14 ounces and wore newborn clothes.

—BRETTE SEMBER
CLARENCE, NEW YORK
👧12 👶6

. . . .

THE BEST PLACE TO GET BOTH MATERNITY CLOTHES and baby clothes are consignment stores. There are good selections and the prices are very reasonable. When you're done with the clothes you can just bring them back to the store for credit and exchange them for other "new" items.

—ANONYMOUS
ALAMEDA, CALIFORNIA
👧7M

DON'T BUY THOSE TEENY-TINY LITTLE SHOES. They're not good for helping your baby learn to walk.

—RACHEL B.
PHILADELPHIA, PENNSYLVANIA
👶3 👶2

⋯⋯⋯⋯

YOU CAN SAVE A LOT OF MONEY by passing around baby clothes, either as hand-me-downs or temporary loaners, while you wait for the next kid to come along.

—KATRINA CURRIER
SAN FRANCISCO, CALIFORNIA
👶17M

⋯⋯⋯⋯

NEVER BUY CLOTHES THAT YOU THINK YOUR BABY will "fit into later" because that never works. I still have baby clothes with tags on them that I was waiting to put my daughters in. They are teenagers now.

—KAREN
DEER PARK, ILLINOIS
👶13 👶11 👶2

⋯⋯⋯⋯

THERE IS A WEB SITE CALLED FREECYCLE.ORG where people are giving away things for free. All you have to do is go pick it up!

—JESSICA L. DELANEY
JOHNSTOWN, COLORADO
👶4 👶2

MY DAUGHTER WILL ONLY EAT THINGS that I eat. She refuses baby food and she refuses the standard child foods like Cheerios, fries and chicken fingers. But if I'm eating lasagna, she'll happily take a bite; she'll eat part of my burrito, rotisserie chicken, beets, salad, and everything else I make for myself.

—DANIELLE
ORANGE, CALIFORNIA
1

SWITCHING FROM NURSING TO SOLIDS WAS AWFUL. I tried spoon-feeding my son baby food, but he would close his mouth and turn his head away. One day I put some cheerios and carrots and toast on in front of him. He used his hands to feed himself. I realized that my son wanted to do it himself. So I just gave him finger food. He's one now, a good eater and the right weight.

—JILLIAN
TEMPE, ARIZONA
1

MY SON WANTS TO EAT EVERYTHING WE EAT. We go out for Chinese food, and he'll eat hot and spicy dishes, sweet dishes, and fried food. He likes curry from Indian restaurants and even eats sushi. My daughter, on the other hand, is a strictly meat-and-potatoes and, occasionally, chicken-nugget kind of girl.

—ANONYMOUS
DALLAS, TEXAS
3 2

Introduce textured foods as soon as you can, like Cheerios, or soft flaky salmon, or juicy summer fruits. This will prevent them from being picky eaters.

—DANIELA
CORTE MADERA,
CALIFORNIA
5 3

WHEN MY SON WAS AROUND SIX WEEKS OLD, he had acid reflux and preferred to be upright as much as possible. At the time he would only sleep about a half hour at a time on his back. Even at night, I was lucky to get an hour and a half out of him. I was told to elevate one end of his crib to help him sleep. This didn't work at all, he simply slid down to one end of the crib. I decided to put my son in his infant car seat and place it in the crib. It worked like a charm!

—SHEENA KROCK
KUNKLETOWN, PENNSYLVANIA
14M

• • • • • • • •

MY YOUNGEST IS THE PICKIEST EATER. One week all he would eat was cut-up sweet potatoes and cheese; after a few days, he refused both those things. The next week, all he would eat was cut-up fruit; after about a week of that, he started spitting everything out. I started putting a variety of cut-up foods on his tray, then ignored him; I didn't try to get him to eat. Eventually, he started eating more foods. Remember that everything is new to them. Just keep offering them a wide variety of foods and let them choose.

—ANONYMOUS
HOUSTON, TEXAS
7   3

Don't panic when your child is sick. When my son got croup, I didn't know it was a fairly simple thing. It sounded so scary, but it wasn't so bad.

—JULIE
FORT COLLINS,
COLORADO
8

I NEVER TOLD ANYONE that I fed my little girl peanut butter. Peanuts and babies together often lead to a trip to the emergency room. I knew she wasn't supposed to have them, but I just wasn't thinking. If I ever told my husband, I think he'd have my head.

—ANONYMOUS
LAS VEGAS, NEVADA
2

My son likes to take nori seaweed, wrap it around a banana, and then eat it. He can eat a whole package of seaweed and about four bananas in one sitting

—ANONYMOUS
MOBILE, ALABAMA
4 1

WE USED TO FEED MY SON FROM OUR PLATES. He would sit in his high chair and we would break off pieces of whatever we were eating and put it on his plate. We were so amazed by how much he would eat, and eat, and eat. I've never seen a baby eat so much food in my life.

—ANONYMOUS
BURBANK, CALIFORNIA
2 6

UNORTHODOX FOOD CHOICES

MY SON USED TO PICK HIS NOSE, show me his findings, and then eat them. It was the grossest thing ever, but I couldn't get him to stop. Eventually he stopped eating them; he just collected his boogers in a bowl by his bed.

—ANONYMOUS
DETROIT, MICHIGAN
👶2 👧5

. . . .

WE LIVE BY THE BEACH, and my son loves eating the sand. He piles it into his mouth handfuls at a time and sometimes he even gets on all fours, puts his mouth to the ground, and starts eating. I try my best to stop him.

—JILLIAN
SAN DIEGO, CALIFORNIA
👶2

. . . .

MY SON LIKES TO EAT FOOD after he throws it on the floor and mashes it with his feet. He then picks up the stepped-on food and puts it in his mouth. It is the vilest thing I've ever seen, but for a while if I hadn't let him eat like that, he wouldn't have eaten at all.

—ANONYMOUS
AUSTIN, TEXAS
👶3 👶1

WHEN MY DAUGHTER WAS ALMOST A YEAR OLD we took her with us to a French restaurant. I ordered a meat dish and my husband ordered fish. The chef made something mild and fried for my daughter. She didn't like it and decided to try our food. She loved both dishes and finished them both. She ate so much of our meals that my husband and I made a second dinner for ourselves when we got home.

—ANONYMOUS
HOLLYWOOD, FLORIDA
👶 3 👶 1

. . . .

MY DAUGHTER WOULDN'T EAT ANYTHING but junk food. Then I found a cookbook called *Sugar-Free Toddlers*, and I have been cooking from it ever since. It has recipes for banana bread, smoothies, and sugar-free cookies. My daughter loves it all; it was such a relief.

—ANONYMOUS
LOS ANGELES, CALIFORNIA
👶 3

. . . .

MY DAUGHTER IS NOW EIGHT MONTHS OLD and still eating baby food. But one day she got tired of watching me eat my buffalo wings—as I was taking a bite, she came in real fast and tried to bite into the other side. It was so funny and cute. She had ranch dressing all over her face.

—CRYSTAL GALE WELLS
MERRILLVILLE, INDIANA
👶 6 👶 8M

Before running to the hospital whenever your child has the sniffles, first call your grandmother and ask her for advice.

—ANDREA PARKER
CHICAGO, ILLINOIS
👶 5

THE FIRST TIME I GAVE MY SON CHOCOLATE I thought I saw his eyes roll back into his head—he was completely possessed. He had the biggest smile on his face! He started spinning around the room like a crazy person, making sounds I'd never heard from him before. It was one of the funniest things I ever saw in my life.

—LINDA
MINNEAPOLIS, MINNESOTA
🍎2

. . . .

MY SON GOES THROUGH PERIODS, two months at a time, where he eats practically nothing. Then for the next two weeks he'll eat everything in the house. Don't stress about it unless your doctor tells you the baby's not at a healthy weight.

—AMANDA
SANTA MONICA, CALIFORNIA
👶3 👩1

. . . .

MY DAUGHTER IS THE PICKIEST EATER—I get so jealous when I see other babies eating whatever they are fed. For breakfast, the only thing she will eat is cheese. I've tried eggs, toast, waffles, cereal—all she wants is cheese. And she won't eat it at the table; she will only eat it off the kitchen floor. I have to break off pieces of cheese and let her eat it off the floor.

—ANONYMOUS
CARLSBAD, CALIFORNIA
👶3 👩1

ALL FALL DOWN

ONE OF THE BIGGEST MISTAKES I made was when I left her on the couch and went into the kitchen to fix her a bottle. As soon as I left the room, she tumbled of off the couch onto the floor. All I could do was run to her rescue, pick her up, and apologize over and over again. Ever since then, I have never left her on the couch without pillows right underneath the couch.

—AMBER WILLIAMSON
COVINGTON, GEORGIA
1

• • • • • • • •

I WAS SO TIRED ONE NIGHT that I plopped my baby down on the couch next to me to chill and watch television. I ended up falling asleep and waking up to a big thump; my baby, falling on the floor.

—GINA
HOUSTON, TEXAS
2

• • • • • • • •

I WAS TAKING MY BABY OUT OF THE CAR ONE DAY, and dropped him. He landed flat on his face. The good news was, he recovered very quickly.

—ANONYMOUS
LAGUNA BEACH, CALIFORNIA
2

MY DAUGHTER WAS JUST STARTING TO CRAWL. I was doing laundry, and I put her in my bed while I changed loads. While I was in the laundry room I heard a loud thump, and I ran back into the bedroom. She had fallen off the bed while trying to reach for a piece of chocolate on the bedside table. Fortunately, she was fine, but it could have been a lot worse.

—ANONYMOUS
LOS ANGELES, CALIFORNIA
3

- - - - - - - - -

MY DAUGHTER FELL DOWN THE STAIRS just a couple of days after she learned to crawl. I knew she was some-what mobile, but I had no idea she could move that fast. I saw her headed for the stairs and tried to catch her, only to miss her by inches as she tumbled down. Luckily, she was fine, but I was a wreck! I cried all night, and made sure to never even let that kind of accident be a possibility ever again.

—ELIZABETH STOUT
CINCINNATI, OHIO
3

ONCE THEY WERE READY FOR SOLID FOOD, I started out feeding my babies every fruit and vegetable possible, and I made sure to do it consistently. Then, when they started eating finger foods, they always ate the fruits and vegetables off their trays first. I think having that consistent approach and sticking with the program helped them to be good, healthy eaters, even as infants.

—BETSY
CINCINNATI, OHIO
😊5 😊1 👶3

• • • • • • • •

MY BABY ONCE ATE SOME GLUE. I was making him a bottle and he grabbed a refrigerator magnet. It went right into his mouth, and the magnet came off the little bobble, and he ate the glue. I called Poison Control and it turned out that there was no harm done: if the glue is dry, it's not toxic.

—CHANDRA MCNICHOLAS
LOS ANGELES, CALIFORNIA
😊1

• • • • • • • •

I TOOK THIS BEAUTIFUL PICTURE OF MY SON when he was 10 months old. He was lying across a hammock and smiling away. Seconds after the shutter snapped, he inched forward, flipped over the hammock and fell to the ground! It turned out he was fine, but now, every time I look at that sweet picture, I remember that horrible moment.

—J.R.M.
CREVE COEUR, MISSOURI
😊19 👶20 👶17 👶9

Instead of baby-proofing my home to the max, I taught my daughter what she could and could not touch.

—ANONYMOUS
DECATUR,
GEORGIA
👶2

TROUBLE BEHIND

I TRIED EVERYTHING TO TREAT my baby's diaper rash: applying Desitin, leaving him with his pants off all the time, changing his formula. Finally, at 11 months, he was put on milk with acidophilus yeast culture and that did the trick—no more red bottom!

—CATHY
GLENCOE, MISSOURI
 14 17

. . . .

IF NOTHING IS WORKING to relieve your baby's diaper rash, believe it or not, it might be strep. And the swimming pool is a breeding ground for it. One of the boys had strep throat and I mentioned to the doctor that the girls had been taking swim lessons and had sore butts, so the doctor swabbed their booties and found strep there!

—TAMI HANFORD
BRIDGETON, MISSOURI
8 7 5 3

WHEN MY DAUGHTER STARTED EATING SOLIDS, the only thing she would eat was Greek olives. I tried everything. For three weeks, she lived on olives. I took her to the doctor: her weight was fine, and he didn't seem to be too concerned. He just told us to keep putting a variety of foods in front of her. Eventually she picked up a fish stick. She thought it was good, and from that moment on we never had food issues again.

—MARLA
BURBANK, CALIFORNIA
3 1

• • • • • • • •

MY WIFE HAD TO GO OUT OF TOWN when our son was four months old and don't you know it—the kid decides to get sick and keep me up all night. I gave him some Tylenol; that didn't work at all. I tried to bring him into bed with me; no luck. The little guy just kept screaming. This went on until about five-thirty in the morning. He slept for about two hours, and then started the party all over again.

—ANONYMOUS
ST. LOUIS, MISSOURI
5 2

Your Little Genius: Walking, Talking & Learning

Growth and development among children is not a competition! Resist the temptation to compare your baby with others (even though you are sure you are raising a genius). Babies grow, develop, and obtain certain developmental milestones at their own pace and in their own time. A normal baby may roll over from front to back at three months or five months. Both are normal. Front-to-back rolling *usually precedes back-to-front rolling, but not always. Some babies sit without support at five months and some at seven to eight months of age. Again, both are normal. Some babies walk at nine or ten months, but the average is 14 months. You can see that the variations in normal development are great. If you are concerned that your child's development may be abnormal, consult your pediatrician.*

I KNEW MY SON WAS SPECIAL when the nurse said that he was the only baby in the hospital nursery who watched her as she moved around the room; she said it was unnerving to be observed by so young a baby.

—JANNY TANG
SANTA CRUZ, CALIFORNIA
31

READ ALL THE BABY BOOKS WITH A GRAIN OF SALT and with the knowledge that your child probably isn't going to fit into whatever model they are espousing. I've noticed they are usually a little more advanced than your baby should or will be at a particular time. They start talking about sleep training at three months, when it's close to impossible before six months; one book mentions your child saying "no" all the time at 12 months, when most babies haven't spoken their first words yet; they speak of reading your child a bedtime story, but this is hard to do before they are about 10 months old, because they just want to eat the book.

—BARBARA MCGLAMERY

MY GIRL'S FIRST WORD WAS "SHOE." She used to look at her shoes in awe; one day she just blurted out the word. She's six now and still fascinated with shoes.

—ANONYMOUS
BURBANK, CALIFORNIA
2 6

WHEN YOUR CHILD IS LEARNING TO WALK, cheer him on. Those first steps are a very magical moment, for both you and your baby. When they take those first steps, they get as excited as you do—they clap and smile. We encourage them through positive reinforcement.

—ALANA SIMMS
FORT COLLINS, COLORADO
👩4 👶1

DON'T PUT YOUR BABY ON A SCALE—like, all one-year-olds need to be walking. My nephew was tested for being slow because he hadn't started walking at 12 months. He was just fine; he walked at 13 months. He just didn't have a reason to do it yet. The other kids were bringing him stuff.

—CATHERINE GRINDA
ATASCOSA, TEXAS
👶-👩-👶16M

TO TEACH YOUR BABY TO WALK, sit with them on the floor and give them encouragement. Also, do leg exercises—it will make them strong. You can stand them on your legs and put them on their backs. Then you grab their ankles and push their knees to their tummy. I did this, and my daughter walked at 10 months and my son at 11 months.

—GLORIA A. SOLIS
SAN ANTONIO, TEXAS
👩15 👶12

WE READ PICTURE BOOKS TO MY GRANDSON all the time. I would take my finger and trace the letters. I would use my finger to count the butterflies on the page. It helps your baby focus on the page.

—J.K. DaPrato
Vancouver, Washington
🐾 36 🐣 33

• • • • • • • •

DON'T WORRY SO MUCH about what other people consider "normal." My son didn't walk till he was nearly two and everybody kept telling me it wasn't normal and that I should be worried. When he finally did take his first step, he pretty much got up and walked across the room. He ended up being a track star.

—Bonnie Dulfon
Boston, Massachusetts
🐣 42 🐾 41 🐾 36

• • • • • • • •

MY DAUGHTER WAS ON THE LATE SIDE for walking; at 15 months she still just didn't seem to care about it. Then one day, that all changed. I had ordered her a pair of sneakers on eBay, and when she saw them she immediately grabbed the shoe laces, stood up and started jiggling them up and down. Eureka! The advantage of standing upright! Hands are available! She took several steps just while playing with the shoes, and she never looked back.

—Cathy C.
Biddeford, Maine
🐾 4

WHEN BABY FALLS ...

IT'S HARD TO WATCH YOUR CHILD FALLING and hitting her head when she's little, but kids' bodies are made for that. When they learn to walk, they fall. You've got to watch out for sharp corners far more than just a simple "thud" onto the ground.

—N. CLARK
HOUSTON, TEXAS
15

• • • • • • • •

MY NATURAL REACTION WAS TO RUN OVER, pick up my daughter when she fell and ask her, "Are you OK?" Like a switch being thrown, she'd start crying. One time I saw her fall. She couldn't see me in the other room. I stood there to see what she was going to do. She got up like nothing happened. So after that, I'd still be concerned when she fell. But if I saw her get up and start looking around for me, I wouldn't acknowledge that she fell. Half the time—if not more than that—she wouldn't cry.

—JOHN D'EREDITA
SYRACUSE, NEW YORK
19   12

WHEN YOUR BABY IS OLD ENOUGH to keep his or her head up, read to them. I propped them on my lap and started reading books. That increased their ability to speak and under- stand language. When they were two, they were already speaking in phrases.

    —JOBETH MCLEOD
    SAN ANTONIO, TEXAS
    26   18

* * * * * * * *

KIDS WALK WHEN THEY ARE READY, talk when they are ready, potty train when they are ready, etc. We don't need to worry about these developmental milestones, compare our kids to others, or try to speed these things along. That just makes the parents nuts and makes the child feel inadequate.

    —ANONYMOUS
    SAN ANTONIO, TEXAS
    9   6

INFANT INFO

Some parents tend to be too overbearing on their newborns. Excessive parental concern may impede a child's language development.

PROVIDE YOUR CHILD WITH PEERS to learn from. With my brother's triplets, each one watches everything the others do. Once one started crawling, the others watched with amazement. Within a month, they were all crawling.

—CATHERINE GRINDA
ATASCOSA, TEXAS
👶-👶-👶 16M

• • • • • • • •

Don't use baby talk. You're teaching your child how to talk, modeling how words are supposed to sound. If you speak in a sing-song fashion, that's how your child will learn to speak.

—SARA
ST. LOUIS PARK, MINNESOTA
👶 4 👶 2

• • • • • • • •

"TOUCHDOWN" WAS MY SON'S FIRST WORD! He said it while watching football one evening. He threw his hands up just like the refs and screamed it out as loud as he could, and the funny thing was the Falcons had just scored!

—TENESHA N. BENTON
STOCKBRIDGE, GEORGIA
👶 6

THE MOST EXCITING PART OF A CHILD'S development is when they start talking. I was surprised that my children knew so many words. We played the game, "What does the dog, cat, cow say," and my children knew all of the animal sounds. It's fascinating how children retain words and information, from hearing adult dialogue to watching television.

—NARY BA
ANTIOCH, CALIFORNIA
3 2

. . . .

TALK TO YOUR BABY AND TELL HER what you're doing. That's what I do: "Hi Emily, I'm going to pick you up now." Or, "Emily, Mommy's going to bathe you now." It may seem very simple, but somehow it seems she's beginning to anticipate actions based on my tone or my sentence. There's recognition.

—M.B.
NEW YORK, NEW YORK
7M

. . . .

ELIZABETH GRACE HAS BEEN SITTING to "read" books since an early age, turning pages and intently looking at photos. We even noticed that she always holds the books right-side up and never upside down. She's absolutely fascinated by them; a future librarian? Maybe!

—AMY SANDLING CRAWFORD
PLANO, TEXAS
1

My daughter took her first steps when we were on vacation in Bar Harbor, Maine, and I'm pretty sure I'll never forget every last detail.

—KEITH REGAN
GRAFTON,
MASSACHUSETTS
5 3

WHEN MY DAUGHTER STARTED to learn to walk, we bought this huge pad that wrapped around our coffee table in the living room. It was designed to cover the corners, but it was always sagging in one area, and it was probably the ugliest thing we could put in our living room. And it was all for naught—one day my daughter was standing at a nearby chair and decided to make the trek to the table, but halfway there she stumbled. Of course, the one part of the table that wasn't covered by that sagging, ugly pad was the corner where she fell and met it with her forehead. She got a nice goose egg from that, but she was OK. And the pad was immediately removed and tossed in the trash.

—JWAIII
ATLANTA, GEORGIA
5 2

• • • • • • • •

MY GRANDSON STARTED WALKING at about a year and a half. He had been crawling for some time and pulling himself up, but not walking. Then one day while he was with my daughter at a library, he just stood up and walked away, as if he had been doing it for weeks. I told my daughter he was probably practicing when no one was watching!

—JOHN R. BRIGHT
ALLENTOWN, PENNSYLVANIA
33 31

BABIES LOVE YOGA. Even before they're old enough to do it themselves, they love watching their moms do it—all the stretching and moving is interesting to them. I teach Mommy/Baby yoga classes, and I think babies can absorb some good habits about breathing and stretching and caring for body and spirit by starting yoga early.

—ELISE COLLINS
SAN FRANCISCO, CALIFORNIA
5

• • • • • • • •

MY DAUGHTER'S FIRST WORD, believe it or not, was, "fucking go!" I didn't realize it but when I drive, I honk my horn and say those same words. Most parents get to brag about their kid's first words. I, on the other hand, had to cower in embarrassment.

—ANONYMOUS
SANTA FE, NEW MEXICO
3

INFANT INFO

When asked which comforting ritual was the hardest to break, 38 percent of parents said giving baby pacifier, 35 percent said rocking baby to sleep, 12 percent chose soothing baby with food, and 15 percent admitted all of the above.

HAPPY FIRST BIRTHDAY!

THE FIRST BIRTHDAY PARTY is more for the parents than the child. The fun really starts at the second birthday.

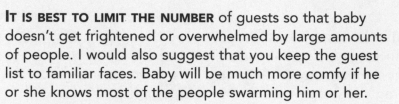

> —LYNDA DIFRANCESCO
> RALEIGH, NORTH CAROLINA
> 👶2 👶2M

• • • • • • • • •

IT IS BEST TO LIMIT THE NUMBER of guests so that baby doesn't get frightened or overwhelmed by large amounts of people. I would also suggest that you keep the guest list to familiar faces. Baby will be much more comfy if he or she knows most of the people swarming him or her.

> —ERIN CALLAHAN
> KERSHAW, SOUTH CAROLINA
> 👶2

• • • • • • • • •

SMALL FAMILY GATHERINGS WORK GREAT for first birthdays. For both of my daughters' first birthdays, I made each their own small chocolate cake and I just let them go to town. Boy, did they love that! Just simple, fun celebrations with close relatives, lots of balloons, and lots of photos.

> —TINA SMITH
> FORT COLLINS, COLORADO
> 👧4 👧2

WE HAD A HUGE FIRST BIRTHDAY for our first son, because we thought he was a miracle, since we thought we couldn't have any children. Then, miracle two came along. His party will be big (because we want to be fair), but not as big.

—MICHELLE M.
OOSTBURG, WISCONSIN
👶2 👶2M

• • • • • • • •

WHEN PLANNING A FIRST BIRTHDAY PARTY, delegate jobs. Have someone in charge of picking up the cake, helping with food, taking pictures, etc. You want to enjoy the party and not run around the whole time.

—BRYNN CYNOR
BUFFALO GROVE, ILLINOIS
👶1

• • • • • • • •

I WAS ACTUALLY VERY BLUE on my son's first birthday because he seemed to be growing so fast!

—D.
COLUMBUS, OHIO
👶7 👧4M

INTERACT WITH YOUR BABY BY SINGING, reading, and talking to them on a daily basis. It's a proven fact that these things help babies with their language development. I'll sometimes talk to my daughter about my day at work. True, she won't understand much of what I'm saying, but she'll soon come to realize that words have meaning.

—EDWARD BARINQUE
EWA BEACH, HAWAII
7M

• • • • • • • • •

MY SON'S FIRST WORD WAS, "OH DEAR!" I think he got that from my wife. Whenever she drops something she says it. I remember, he was playing with a toy and dropped it. He immediately looked up and said, "Oh, dear!"

—RICK
HOUSTON, TEXAS
1

• • • • • • • • •

READING TO CHILDREN IS SO IMPORTANT. My two older girls were toddlers when my third daughter was a baby, so I read to them every time I nursed the baby. That became our routine. We had an overstuffed rocking chair, and while I sat there, each one would sit on an arm of the chair. As I rocked the baby and read, they were being rocked, too. It was wonderful.

—MARY LOBUE
LAS VEGAS, NEVADA
48 46 44

MY LITTLE GIRL HAS A RUBBER DUCK with a hole in it. She puts it in the water, then brings it up to her mouth and drinks from it. Most babies her age couldn't figure that out. She essentially knows that water goes in a cup and she designed her own cup with the duck!

—ANONYMOUS
HOLLYWOOD, FLORIDA.
👧3 👧1

• • • • • • • • •

I ENJOYED READING TO MY SONS when they were little. Even though I knew they didn't know what I was reading or saying, I still felt in my heart that reading to them showed them love. I would always read them poems by Langston Hughes, Gwendolyn Brooks, Countee Cullen, and other African American poets. I would even read speeches by Martin Luther King Jr., and Malcolm X so they would have an early understanding of how talented, and strong African American men spoke and how they too can become powerful and change the world. I think it helped because all of my sons never had problems with the law, and they are all in school pursuing their dreams.

—BEATRICE CHAPPELL
CHICAGO, ILLINOIS
👦26 👦19 👦18

Teaching a baby sign language helps them communicate earlier, and it won't hurt their regular language development.

—K.C.
SAN FRANCISCO,
CALIFORNIA
👶?

ONE DAY, WHEN OUR SON was 11 months old, our three-year-old daughter left her puzzle on the floor. I told her, "If you leave it there, he'll eat it!" She didn't pick it up. Later, we walked by the room and he was putting together the last piece of the puzzle. We couldn't believe it. Mean parents that we were, we dumped it and made him do it again. And he did! Our son is off the charts now in math and science. He'll probably be an engineer.

—CHERYL NORTON
WASHOUGAL, WASHINGTON
13 11

. . . .

MY DAUGHTER'S FIRST WORD WAS "CLOCK". She pointed at a clock and just said it. We were shocked! I figured, well, at least she'll be on time everywhere she goes.

—ANONYMOUS
CONYERS, GEORGIA
16 13 10 18

. . . .

EVEN BEFORE MY DAUGHTERS were old enough to understand what I was saying, I started reading to them.
We had a great bedtime routine: I would give them their bottles, then their baths, and then I'd rock them in the rocking chair and read. Now, both of my daughters are reading on their own, and they love it!

—DONNA
ALLENTOWN, PENNSYLVANIA
7 6

NO BABY TALK

If you want children to learn how to speak intelligently, you must speak properly to them. When my daughter was born, I would speak to her as if we were in a meeting, and I was the one trying to propose a deal to her. I would use intellectual language just to change her diaper. I once said, "Young lady, you must always learn how to have good hygiene, and soiling your garments are not the best way to practice such behavior." She looked at me and laughed. But I know my adult talk worked because my daugher's first real word besides "dada," "mama," and "baba," was "achieve." I'm sure it was all the times I told her she could achieve all her goals if she just worked hard that made her say that word. But my mother, who was in the room when she said "achieve," said my daughter really said "a cheese." But, of course, I don't believe it— even if I was eating some Swiss cheese atthe moment.

—LINDA STOVALL
WESTCHESTER, ILLINOIS
5

SEE HOW THEY GROW

A good example of why things happen when they do: At birth, a baby's focal length (the distance at which vision is best) is exactly the distance between the baby's eyes and the mother's face while nursing. Another example: Most babies calm when hearing their parents' voices—more than upon hearing any other voice. Isn't that wonderful planning?

Generally, babies develop strength and coordination from top to bottom. Head control happens before core (trunk) strength, which develops before leg coordination. Therefore, your baby will have control over his arms and hands before his legs and feet. That's why babies scoot using their hands and arms and drag their bottoms and legs. They sit before they stand; they cruise before they walk. See, it's easy! The timing and pace of this developmental continuum varies greatly. Some children walk at nine months and some at 16 months; both can be normal. Just sit back and enjoy the changes, which can seem to occur daily.

WHEN MY BABY WAS EIGHT MONTHS OLD we put different colored blocks around the living room. We would say the name of a color to her and she would crawl to that corresponding block and pick it up. It was amazing, because she never messed up.

—ANONYMOUS
LAS VEGAS, NEVADA
2

. . . .

MY FIRST SON'S FIRST WORD WAS "TRUCK," but we thought he was saying, you know, that famous curse word that starts with the letter F. We finally put two and two together when he pointed to a picture of a truck. My second son hasn't said anything yet, but we are anxiously waiting.

—ANONYMOUS
AUSTIN, TEXAS
3 1

. . . .

MY LITTLE GIRL PICKED UP THE NEWSPAPER one day and opened it up as if she was intensely reading an article. From that moment we knew she would be smart and curious. We started telling all of our friends that are little girl could read and was interested in current events. She's four now and she asks me to read her articles from the paper.

—ANONYMOUS
NEW YORK, NEW YORK
4

Sing to your baby. I exposed my children to all kinds of music. Now when they hear old songs they think they've never heard before they still know all the words.

—JOBETH MCLEOD
SAN ANTONIO, TEXAS
26 18

I WONDER IF FIRST WORDS PREDICT THE FUTURE. My daughter's first word was "bye-bye." Not too long after that, she began "running away" on a regular basis, taking her Barbie suitcase with her.

—N.L.
ST. LOUIS, MISSOURI
👦19 👦17 👧22

- - - - - - - - -

MY CHILD'S FIRST WORD WAS "DADDY," and that was a little awkward for me because his father was not living with us. I was feeling like, he sees me 24/7; why can't I get the first word? Why couldn't it have been "mommy"?

—AMBUR BANNER
COLUMBUS, OHIO
👦2

- - - - - - - - -

I'D ALWAYS LOVED RAP MUSIC AND HIP-HOP, but I believe that is too adult for babies and children to listen too. I wanted my child to grow up listening to gospel, or even classical music. I bought a Stravinsky CD and started playing it for my baby. It would calm her down and help her fall asleep. But I started to enjoy the music, too, so I bought more CDs. Some artsy friends of mine told me to get Vivaldi and Bach; I loved them all. I saved some money for a year's worth of violin lessons. Now classical music is my favorite.

—TAMEKA SMITH
CHICAGO, ILLINOIS
👦12 👧13

My second child's first word was "French fry."

—SHAWNA N. RUSSELL
SACRAMENTO, CALIFORNIA
👦10 👦4
👧3

More Wisdom: Good Stuff that Doesn't Fit Anywhere Else

It's been an amazing first year. Your baby and you are very different beings then you were one year ago. Your baby has developed from a totally dependent infant to a mostly coordinated one-year-old. Birth weight has tripled, length has increased by one third, and the body is beginning to catch up with head size. Feeding has become more coordinated (and more messy) as your baby wants to do more things independently. He or she is probably up on her feet and cruising around with the support of furniture or other objects. About six teeth have erupted, with more to come. A few sounds that *may be words are developing. The first year challenges have been met and accomplished and you are looking forward to new and interesting ones during the second year. Walking and talking will be among the highlights.*

You are now an accomplished parent with increasing confidence in your skills. You are still delighted as your baby seems to develop a new skill almost daily. You are probably getting more rest and are more comfortable getting away from your baby because you have confidence in your chosen caregivers. Your life is gradually getting back to "normal," although it will never be the same as it was before pregnancy. Your priorities have changed and your baby is now your most important one. You can't believe that you could love any little being so much, and even that increases with each passing day.

Congratulations, you made it!

HAVING KIDS IS THE MOST AMAZING, scary, frustrating, wonderful, huge love that you're ever going to go through for the rest of your life.

—K.J.
ST. AUGUSTINE, FLORIDA
👶 6 👶 1

• • • • • • • •

I HAVE HAD FIVE KIDS. When you have more than one, you realize that the stages you thought would never end actually will. The first time around, you think your kid will never sleep through the night or ever be potty trained. But by the fifth kid, you know the stages of development well. So I would advise new parents to study the stages of development and realize that all things will pass. This will minimize panic and allow you to relax more.

—A.M.
PASSAIC, NEW JERSEY
😊 12 😊 10 😊 8 😊 6 😊 3

• • • • • • • •

FOCUS ON YOUR RELATIONSHIP with your spouse or partner as much as or more than you focus on your relationship with your child. Children who live with happy grown-ups who express love for one another learn to be happy children who express love for one another. I read that what a child needs most is a cheerful care provider. I really think this is true.

—S.C.
PORTLAND, MAINE
👶–👶 5 😊 1

> *Kiss your babies a ton. They will grow up to be affec-tionate!*
>
> —STEPH D.
> BALTIMORE,
> MARYLAND
> 👶 18 😊 15
> 👶 13

KIDS CHANGE CONSTANTLY, and their care needs do as well. When we raised our kids, of course, there were difficult times. But we always had faith that if we planted the right values, they would sprout. And they have.

—S.S.
PASSAIC, NEW JERSEY

• • • • • • • •

One time we brought our son to the doctor with a complaint. I asked if we needed a prescription. The doctor said, 'Yes,' and wrote one. It read, 'Reassurance.' That's all we needed!

—DEANA KRAUSE
CHICAGO, ILLINOIS
11 9

• • • • • • • •

KIDS REACT TO HOW YOU REACT. Stressed out parents equal a stressed child. I'm highly prepared with food, wipes, diapers, toys in the car. I have snacks in my purse, etc.—so that alleviates any panic from being ill-prepared.

—MELISSA STEIN
3

MOMENTS AND MILESTONES

When my first son was born I had to work. I hated having to work, so it was even more devastating when I missed a milestone. One day I got a call from my sitter telling me that my son had rolled over. I was crushed; I had missed a "first". When I got pregnant with my second son, I was able to quit and stay home. After he was born, I knew that I would never miss another "first." So there I was one night, listening to him cooing in his crib. When I went to check on him, he had rolled over! I had missed another child's first rollover! This wasn't supposed to happen! I realized that it is not that important that you are there for every "first," as long as you are there and present in your child's life. We may not see all the first walks, first kicks, or hear the first words, but when you are there with your child, it is important to make the moments count. Don't worry about the first moments, worry about moments.

—TERRI A. MILLARD
HAMILTON, OHIO
9 5

EVERYTHING THAT YOU CAN PUT INTO your children is an investment for the future, whether you know it or not. It will come back to you tenfold when they are adults.

—BRIAN COY
EL CAJON, CALIFORNIA
👶23 👶21

· · · · · · · · ·

THE MORE TIME YOU GIVE THEM AS KIDS, the less time they'll spend in a shrink's office when they're older. Don't think that buying them presents is a substitute for being there with them—it's not. There is no real substitute for parents.

—ANONYMOUS
BETHESDA, MARYLAND
👶9 👶6

· · · · · · · · ·

IT IS SO EASY TO GET CAUGHT up in everything that you need to do for baby on a daily basis—changing diapers, feeding, changing and washing clothes, getting them down for naps, etc.—that you can miss out on precious moments. Appreciate every second with the baby. They are only that age once. If the laundry piles up because you want to cuddle with the baby, then so be it.

—BARB G.
PITTSBURGH, PENNSYLVANIA
👶9 👶2

Love them a lot. Just love them all the time and that's pretty much it.

*—TERI
SEATTLE,
WASHINGTON
👶12 👶8*

WRITE A LETTER TO YOUR CHILD EVERY YEAR that tells them about all the important events that have gone on in their lives. This gives him or her a connection to family. I keep records of things like where we went on vacation, what my daughter's favorite toys were, and who was her boyfriend. I lost my mom when I was 14, and I don't know about a lot of my childhood. Writing a letter each year lets my children know how important they are to me.

> —S.F.
> SAN ANTONIO, TEXAS
> 👶20 👶16

Sleep while you can. And carry Handi-Wipes.

—JENNIFER
LAWLER
LAWRENCE,
KANSAS
👶7

. . . .

HOW DID I SURVIVE THE FIRST YEAR of being the single mother of twins? I was naïve. Being in this situation for the first time, I didn't know what to expect, so I didn't realize the enormous effort that I had made until long after I made it. I was so busy "doing" that there was no time to reflect, think about the future, etc. All I could do was deal with the moment.

> —NANCY LOU W.
> LITTLE SILVER, NEW JERSEY
> 👶-👶5

. . . .

ALWAYS CARRY A PLASTIC BAG WITH YOU. You never know when you'll get a half-chewed graham cracker or dirty diaper that needs to be disposed of.

> —LORI B.
> CHARLESTON, SOUTH CAROLINA
> 👶19 👶16 👶13 👶3

THE TAO OF PARENTHOOD

I spent a large part of my 20s searching for spiritual truth, awakening, maybe enlightenment even. I learned to meditate, practice yoga, demand discipline and honor respect. But nothing compares to the daily spiritual practice that I experience with my children. You've heard it before—children are our best teachers. Well, I have three wild, funny, lovable Buddhas who teach me everyday. If you think you know what your children need, well, you're missing the great opportunity. The real lesson is not about how you will discipline them, get them to eat their vegetables or stay in their bed at night. The real lesson is in letting go of the chaos of motherhood—finding your true self, your inner calm, when life is swirling by you.

At the park the other day I was holding conversations with two different mothers, pushing my seven-month-old in her stroller while chasing my two-year-old so I could change his poopy diaper, and keeping an eye out for my three-year-old who had run off in another direction to look for a caterpillar he named Bobby. No, I don't have time these days to be searching for enlightenment in lotus atop a mountain, but I don't really have the need to, either. I have just what I need to make me a better person right here in front of me.

—JULIE WARNER MICCICHI
ATLANTA, GEORGIA
😊4 😊2 👶7M

NEW PARENTS ARE SO WRAPPED UP in "the first time my baby did this, the first time they did that, etc." But it's also important to remember that things will—and do—change. Try to think about "the last time my baby took a bottle" and "the last time my baby wore a diaper, slept in a crib, nursed, took a nap, etc." These are important milestones, too!

—WENDY SNYDER
WESTMINSTER, COLORADO
8 4

· · · · · · · · ·

This is not a test. Don't get so caught up in trying to be so perfect that you don't enjoy your baby.

— MELODY PHILLIPS
SARATOGA SPRINGS, NEW YORK
17 16

· · · · · · · · ·

LET THEM RUN AROUND WITH DIFFERENT-COLORED shoes, or no shoes at all. It's OK if they wear clothes that don't match. I just let my two-year-old enjoy being a little girl.

—SHARI LONG, CNM (MIDWIFE)
CHEYENNE, WYOMING
21 19 12 2

I WAS NERVOUS ABOUT EVERYTHING when my first child was born. When my husband and I brought her home from the hospital, I held a tissue up to her nose so she wouldn't breathe in any germs! When I had my son nine-and-a-half years later, it was completely different. When we left the hospital with him, we stopped at McDonald's on the way home! But the good news is that even with these two completely different parenting styles, both of my kids are terrific adults, with successful lives of their own.

—ANONYMOUS
LONG VALLEY, NEW JERSEY
32 23

> *Hug your child at every opportunity and always talk to them in a soothing voice.*
>
> —K.K.
> FALMOUTH,
> MAINE
> 32 29

· · · · · · · · ·

MY BIGGEST SURPRISE about having a baby? Realizing how much I could love someone. Perhaps that sounds corny. But for me, every day was like Christmas with my baby son. I jumped out of bed excited about spending another day with him. I held him for almost the entire first year of his life. That amount of love is overwhelming. No, the feeling does not end. He's 34 now and we're still very close.

—NAN B.
WILLIAMSBURG, VIRGINIA
34

THE THING I WOULD DO DIFFERENTLY if I had it all to do over: I wouldn't worry so much about the mess kids make when they are young. I used to run myself ragged picking up after them constantly. Now I'd just let it be. Who cares?

— CHARLENE DEPASQULE
PITTSBURGH, PENNSYLVANIA
21 18 15

* * * * * * * *

Babies make you younger and older at the same time—younger because you care for them and see things through a child's eyes, and older because you must become more mature and less selfish.

—JENNIFER B.
YARDLEY, PENNSYLVANIA

* * * * * * * *

TEACH YOUR CHILDREN TO BE PASSIONATE when they're little—whether it's about you, a favorite toy, or the movie you've watched a thousand times. When they grow up, that passion will guide them. Support the journey!

—MARY M.
SPRINGFIELD, ILLINOIS
21 17

I CAN REMEMBER MY ONE MOMENT OF PANIC: I couldn't figure out if you take a baby out of the house before or after you feed her. I was so concerned that she would cry in public, and what would I do? I called my sister, who had had her second child six weeks before. She told me later how she chuckled after she got off the phone, because it really didn't matter. And I asked in all seriousness!

—DEBORAH KRUEGER
PORT HURON, MICHIGAN
🧒 30 🧒 24

• • • • • • • • •

JUST LOVE THEM. Everything else comes along and falls into place. They get potty trained. They give up their bottle. In the grand scheme of things, these "milestones" really aren't so important. They happen when they happen. Each child is different, so you have to figure out what each one needs, and then you have to do it. If they need a pacifier or a blanket, let them have it. They'll outgrow these things on their own, in their own time. My daughter gave up her bottle when she was 13 months old. My son had his bottle until he was four years old. Big deal! Now they're both well-adjusted adults. I learned to be flexible when it comes to growth and development.

—ANONYMOUS
FORT COLLINS, COLORADO
🧒 25 👶 18

> *Don't have more than two kids. Once they have you outnumbered you're in trouble.*
>
> —CINDY RODGERS
> PITTSBURGH,
> PENNSYLVANIA
> 👶 17

WORDS TO LIVE BY

When it comes to parenting, the only thing you truly have control over is yourself. Really. You might think you can read a baby book and find a solution to why your three-month-old isn't sleeping through the night like your neighbor's child, but most likely you'll just be disappointed. And we all would like to think that all of our daily efforts will produce the most well-adjusted, caring, responsible 18-year-old who will make honor roll her freshmen year at an Ivy League college while volunteering on weekends to serve soup to the homeless. Que sera sera—whatever will be will be. If you want to give your children a real gift, be true to yourself. Work on becoming the best person you can be. When your children look into the eyes of a confident, powerful and happy human being, they'll know that it is attainable to them.

—JULIE WARNER MICCICHI
ATLANTA, GEORGIA
4 2 7M

IF YOU HAVE A BICULTURAL KID, it's important to keep them connected with both cultures. I think that's especially true if they're biracial, as they will most definitely go through periods where they identify more with one race or the other. Our son considers himself both a white American and Filipino-American, and he knows a lot about both cultures.

—JULIE
SAN FRANCISCO, CALIFORNIA
👁13

DADS, IF YOU'RE GOING TO SHAVE off facial hair, do it just a little bit day by day, and let the baby watch you. My eight-month-old daughter screamed the first time she saw me after I shaved off my beard. She cried every time she looked at me for days and was terrified of me.

—JACK MORRIS
BOSTON, MASSACHUSETTS
👁42 41 36

PARENTHOOD CAN BRING OUT THE BEST and the worst in you. You have to re-evaluate a lot of things in your life, and you summon this reserve of patience you never entirely knew existed. All of your issues from your own parents come up, and after all the analysis and acknowledging that you want to do a better job than your own parents, you may, ironically, end up parenting like them.

—PAULA FISCHER
SAN JOSE, CALIFORNIA
13 👁12 6

ANYBODY WHO HAS BEEN THROUGH PARENTING has probably learned something that could come in handy to you. Don't dismiss any advice outright. But at the same time everybody has a different idea of how to raise their babies and you may not want to do something just because it worked for someone else. Don't be afraid to try something that you wouldn't ordinarily. You may be pleasantly surprised!

—C.M.
PITTSBURGH, PENNSYLVANIA
19   17

• • • • • • • •

DON'T MISS A THING. Not the first tooth, not the first steps. That is my biggest regret— that I had to work too much. It means a lot for kids to have their parents around. Even if you have to live in a smaller apartment, or never eat out, or share a car: One of you shouldn't work full-time during the early years. You can always go back to a job when they start school.

—JANE POWELL
EARLYSVILLE, VIRGINIA
34   31

• • • • • • • •

HUG AND KISS YOUR KIDS A LOT. Even if you're not normally a hugger, it will eventually feel natural, and it helps you raise really happy kids.

—S.M.P.
PORTLAND, MAINE
12   8

Babies arrive with personalities. Get to know yours.

— MELODY PHILLIPS
SARATOGA SPRINGS, NEW YORK
17   16

READY FOR COLLEGE?

START YOUR COLLEGE FUND EARLY. Compound interest makes it better to save $20 a month from the time your kid is one day old than to save $100 a month starting when they're five. And, there's no such thing as too small an amount. Even if at the end of the year you only have $60, that's still $60.

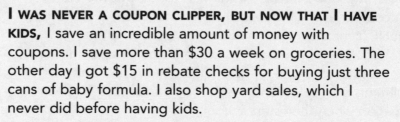

—ROB McHARGUE
SAN ANTONIO, TEXAS
12 11

I WAS NEVER A COUPON CLIPPER, BUT NOW THAT I HAVE KIDS, I save an incredible amount of money with coupons. I save more than $30 a week on groceries. The other day I got $15 in rebate checks for buying just three cans of baby formula. I also shop yard sales, which I never did before having kids.

—SARAH SISSON CHRISTENSEN
SAN DIEGO, CALIFORNIA
2 2M

SET UP A COLLEGE ACCOUNT FOR A NEW BABY as soon as you possibly can. Start early and save, save, save.

—S.M.P.
PORTLAND, MAINE
12 8

MY WIFE AND I WOULD THINK NOTHING of having a four dollar coffee every day but somehow couldn't find any leftover money for college savings. So, we've stopped coffee cold turkey and put eight dollars per day (actually $250 per month) toward her college savings. If we continue for the next 17 years or so, she should have enough to pay for three to four years of a public college or about half of a private college.

—CARL
MINNEAPOLIS, MINNESOTA
1

• • • • • • • •

CHECK IF YOUR EMPLOYER OFFERS a child care flex account. It allows you to take out pre-tax money from your check for child care. That saves money, especially when you have more than one child.

—KRISTI GRAHAM
CHARLOTTE, NORTH CAROLINA
4 1

• • • • • • • •

IF NOTHING ELSE STICKS, KNOW THIS: PAY YOURSELF FIRST.
Put aside one hour's pay a day, and don't touch it, ever.

—SHIRLEY GUTKOWSKI
SUN PRAIRIE, WISCONSIN
26 25 -23 21

AS THE PARENT OF A DISABLED CHILD, the best advice I have for any parent is to be the author of your own expectations. Don't let other people's expectations become yours. No one else can possibly know what my life is like, so their opinions and judgments are absolutely immaterial to me. It's very refreshing for someone who spent too much of her life worrying about what other people think.

—JENNIFER LAWLER
LAWRENCE, KANSAS
6

Don't stress yourself about a clean house and clean children. They can mess it up faster than you can pick it up.

—MARY BECKERING
SYRACUSE, NEW YORK
5 3

TO DRIVE A CAR, YOU NEED A LICENSE, and you need a permit to go fishing or to own a gun. But with children, there are no manuals. Raising children is truly life's greatest responsibility, but the approach is all trial and error.

—PAULA FISCHER
SAN JOSE, CALIFORNIA
13 12 6

THE SWEETEST MOMENTS

THE SWEETEST MOMENT WITH MY KIDS was when my son taught my daughter to take a bottle. My husband and I were trying for over two weeks to get her to suck on it. My son, who was about two at the time, walked over, grabbed the bottle from my husband and held it up for our daughter, and she immediately took it.

—ANONYMOUS
FT. LAUDERDALE, FLORIDA
5 2

MY DAUGHTER AND I FLEW OUT to my mom's wedding. My daughter was just a couple of months old then. My mom took us to the airport and we were waiting for our flight. My mom was holding her and playing with her and that was the very first time she laughed. It was the funniest, cutest sound I'd heard. She was just laughing and laughing.

—LASHAWNA
GRANADA HILLS, CALIFORNIA
8 10

THE SWEETEST MOMENT WITH MY LITTLE GIRL was the first time she hugged me back. I just started crying.

—ANONYMOUS
LAS VEGAS, NEVADA
2

THE SWEETEST MOMENT WITH MY DAUGHTER was the first time she gave me a kiss and a hug. I was feeling a little sad one day, and this little girl, not even two years old, sat on my lap, gave me a kiss and a hug and an "everything is going to be all right" pat on the back.

—ANONYMOUS
SANTA MONICA, CALIFORNIA
👧2

• • • • • • • •

IT WAS IN THE HOSPITAL RIGHT AFTER I had my daughter. After she was cleaned off, I said her name and she opened her eyes like she recognized me already. That was pretty cool.

—CANDACE NICHELLE BRUMFIELD
WEST PALM BEACH, FLORIDA
👧7 👧4 👧1

• • • • • • • •

THE SWEETEST MOMENT WITH BOTH OF MY SONS was when my older son tried to get my younger son to stop crying. My youngest was having a bad day and my eldest went over to him, sat down, hugged him, and kissed his tears.

—LORI
TEMPE, ARIZONA
👦5 👦2

THE FIRST TIME SHE SMILED; I don't think I've ever felt that kind of feeling in my life. What a smile can do from this little, itty-bitty baby is amazing. Yeah, the smile.

—J.V.
LOS ANGELES, CALIFORNIA
1

· · · · · · · ·

THE FIRST TIME THEY SMILE is always great. You suddenly think, "Oh, you're interacting with me and you're not just a blob anymore."

—AMANDA
SANTA MONICA, CALIFORNIA
3 1

· · · · · · · ·

THE FIRST WORD, FROM EACH OF MY DAUGHTERS, was one of my sweetest moments with them, in spite of the fact that they all said "Daddy."

—LILLIE MARIE CUTTER
STONE MOUNTAIN, GEORGIA
37 24 22

MY FAVORITE PIECE OF PARENTING ADVICE came from my mother. When I was pregnant, my mother said, "No matter how hard any parenting stage is, it will always pass. Nothing will last forever." It's so true: Messy eating, diaper changing, and colds and stomach bugs don't last forever. In a few days, weeks, or months each of them will pass. Keeping this advice in mind really helps you get through the tough spots.

—PAULA
NORTHAMPTON, PENNSYLVANIA
3 1

* * * * * * * *

Love them and hold them and believe that you can't spoil them. You just have to keep them warm and safe and fed.

—DEB S.
EL CAJON, CALIFORNIA
22 13

YOU'RE NOT GOING TO GET EVERYTHING DONE on your to-do list—no, the housekeeping won't all get done. At least you vacuumed today; good for you. Now make time to get down on the floor and play with your children. It goes by fast. Make the decision to enjoy your children.

—TORI KOPPELMAA
SAN JOSE, CALIFORNIA
6 - 4 2

* * * * * * * *

MEET OTHER NEW MOMS. The laughter, tears, empathy and friendships will be treasured forever. Don't go it alone. Keep repeating, "I will survive" in your head. Take all of the advice you get and forget 75 percent of it. Then, do it again.

—COURTNEY
OAKLAND, CALIFORNIA
2 1

MY MOTHER, WHO'S STILL ALIVE AT 96, says that a baby should always be wearing a hat to keep it warm. Well, don't let my mother see you, but I think it's OK if the baby is not always covered. They're not that fragile.

—MARY C.
TUCSON, ARIZONA
35 33 31 30

* * * * * * * *

After two boys, to be able to clip a cute little bow—any shape, any color—in my daughter's hair is my absolute favorite thing!

—WENDY
LOVELAND, OHIO
7 5 1

* * * * * * * *

HOLD YOUR CHILDREN A LOT. I've seen the merits of it particularly with my four-year-old granddaughter. She's always been held and hugged a lot, and she's a very happy, social child. Parents used to be told, "Don't hold your children so much, you'll spoil them." That is not true. You can never hold them and love them enough.

—JOYCE
FORT COLLINS, COLORADO
31 29 25 20

I THINK A LOT OF PEOPLE WORRY when they're having a second baby that they couldn't possibly love the second baby as much as they do their first. I know I worried about that. Your first baby is the center of your life. You worry that your second baby will be an interruption. But the amazing thing is, you do love that second baby every single bit as much as the first.

—W.F.
MERTZTOWN, PENNSYLVANIA
24 20

Keep hand and foot prints of your new-born. You'll never believe they were once that small!

—ANONYMOUS
17
14

WHEN YOU'RE A PARENT WITH YOUNG KIDS, you're so busy earning a living, making a home, and raising your kids that you don't have even one second to enjoy those moments. But when you're older, with a little distance, you realize that the brief time your kids are babies is precious.

—ANONYMOUS
LONG VALLEY, NEW JERSEY
32 23

THE BEST ADVICE I EVER GOT after I had my baby was to trust my own instincts. I got so many different views and advice on what I should do with my daughter. But you will know what's right to do. If you feel like it's right—go with it. A lot of that first year is about common sense.

—NIEEMA TURIYA PEYREFITTE
HAWTHORNE, CALIFORNIA
1

SPECIAL THANKS

Thanks to our intrepid "headhunters" for going out to find so many respondents from around the country with interesting advice to share:

Jamie Allen, Chief Headhunter

Paula Andruss
Jennifer Blaise
Helen Bond
Scott Deckman
Elizabeth Edwardsen
Sara Faiwell
Brandi Fowler
Shannon Hurd
Teena Hammond
Lisa Jaffe Hubbell
Natasha Lambropoulos
Nancy Larson
Nicole Lessin
R.M. Lofton
Ken McCarthy
Lindsey Roth Miller

Jennifer Nittoso
Christina Orlovsky
Andrea Parker
Adam Pollock
Peter Ramirez
William Ramsey
Kazz Regelman
Jennifer Bright Reich
Dana Rothblatt
Beth Turney Rutchik
Graciela Sholander
Staci Siegel
Laura Roe Stevens
Jade Walker
Wendy Webb
Jennifer Weiner

Thanks, too, to our editorial advisor, Anne Kostick, and our production editor, Gayle Greene. And thanks to our assistant, Miri Greidi, for her yeoman's work at keeping us all organized. The real credit for this book, of course, goes to all the people whose experiences and collective wisdom make up this guide. There are too many of you to thank individually, but you know who you are.

CREDITS

Page 36: *Family Fun* magazine, 2004.

Page 82: Reuters Health, Charnicia E. Huggins, September 14, 2004.

Page 96: www.todaysmom.com

Page 167: www.todaysmom.com

Page 176: *Family Fun* magazine, 2004.

Page 251: American Academy of Allergy, Asthma and Immunology.

Page 283: *The Late Talker: What to Do if Your Child Isn't Talking Yet,* by Dr. Marilyn C. Agin, Lisa F. Geng and Malcolm J. Nicholl.

Page 287: *Parenting* magazine, October 2004.

Praise for HUNDREDS OF HEADS® *Guides:*

"Hundreds of Heads is an innovative publishing house ... Its entertaining and informative 'How To Survive ...' series takes a different approach to offering advice. Thousands of people around the nation were asked for their firsthand experiences and real-life tips in six of life's arenas. Think 'Chicken Soup' meets 'Zagats,' says a press release, and rightfully so."

—ALLEN O. PIERLEONI
"BETWEEN THE LINES," *THE SACRAMENTO BEE*

"A concept that will be ... a huge seller and a great help to people. I firmly believe that today's readers want sound bytes of information, not tomes. Your series will most definitely be the next 'Chicken Soup.'"

—CYNTHIA BRIAN
TV/RADIO PERSONALITY, BEST SELLING AUTHOR: *CHICKEN SOUP FOR THE GARDENER'S SOUL; BE THE STAR YOU ARE!; THE BUSINESS OF SHOW BUSINESS*

"Move over, 'Dummies'... Can that 'Chicken Soup'! Hundreds of Heads are on the march to your local bookstore!"

—ELIZABETH HOPKINS
KFNX (PHOENIX) RADIO HOST, *THINKING OUTSIDE THE BOX*

"The series ... could be described as 'Chicken Soup for the Soul' meets 'Worst Case Scenario.'"

—RACHEL TOBIN RAMOS
ATLANTA BUSINESS CHRONICLE

Other titles in the HUNDREDS OF HEADS® *series:*

HOW TO SURVIVE YOUR MARRIAGE

"This book is the best wedding present I got! It's great to go into a marriage armed with the advice of hundreds of people who have been through it all already!"

— ANN MEAGHER, MARRIED 2 MONTHS

"Before you wrap up another huge bowl or pair of candlesticks for a wedding present, consider giving the couple something to help ensure they'll use the gifts, not split them up—How to Survive Your Marriage. This is not your typical New Age marriage manual full of psychobabble... it is advice from couples who have been wed for months, years and decades."

— LAURI GITHENS HATCH, DEMOCRAT & CHRONICLE

"What a great idea. My wife and I (95 and 96) don't intend to quit after 71 years of marriage—it's a great institution. This book should help lots of other people match our record."

— DAVID COHEN, EXECUTIVE DIRECTOR,
FRIENDS OF THE QUEENS COLLEGE (NY)
LIBRARY, MARRIED 71 YEARS

"I love this book!"

— LIFETIME RADIO HOST DONNA BRITT

"Simple tricks to help save your marriage."

—WCBS Radio, New York

"Full of honest advice from newlyweds and longtime couples. This book answers the question—'How do other people do it?'"

—Ellen Sabin, MPH, MPA. Executive Director,
The Equality in Marriage Institute

HOW TO LOSE 9,000 LBS. (OR LESS)

"...common-sense advice culled from average dieters...the book doesn't disappoint."

—St. Louis Dispatch

HOW TO SURVIVE YOUR TEENAGER

"...wisdom on each page...provides insight, humor, and empathy..."

—Foreword Magazine

HOW TO SURVIVE A MOVE
"...the wisdom of 600 moving veterans..."

—The Washington Post

"compiles hundreds of essential moving tips, real-life stories, and quotes..."

—Library Journal

BE THE CHANGE!

"This is a book that could change your life. Read the stories of people who reached out to help somebody else and discovered they were their own ultimate beneficiary. It's almost magic and it could happen to everyone. Go!"

—JIM LEHRER
EXECUTIVE EDITOR AND ANCHOR, NEWSHOUR WITH JIM LEHRER

"An inspiring look at the profound power of the individual to make a positive difference in the lives of others. *Be the Change!* is more than an eloquent tribute to volunteer service—it increases awareness of our shared humanity."

—ROXANNE SPILLETT
PRESIDENT, BOYS & GIRLS CLUBS OF AMERICA

"Civic involvement is an enriching joy, as the people in this book make clear. It's also what makes America so great. This is a wonderful and inspiring book."

—WALTER ISAACSON
CEO, ASPEN INSTITUTE

ABOUT THE EDITOR

ROBERT A. MENDELSON, M.D., F.A.A.P., has practiced pediatrics in Portland, Oregon for 43 years. His favorite patients have been the babies of new parents who may be struggling to make sure that everything is perfect during that wonderful first year of life. During his practice, he has always strived to educate new parents to be increasingly self sufficient. As he says: "The more parents know what to expect during that most important first year of life, the more confident and relaxed they will be." He and his wife, a pediatric nurse practitioner, co-authored a book on parenting. They also contributed to the American Academy of Pediatrics, *Caring for Your Baby and Young Child, Birth to Age Five*. Dr. Mendelson is a national media spokesperson for The American Academy of Pediatrics. He frequently appears locally and nationally on radio and television offering parenting advice. He enjoys his four children and eight grandchildren, and playing tennis and golf in the Pacific Northwest.